Comments About Paul Ferrini's Books

I feel that this work comes from a continuing friendship with the deepest part of the Self. I trust its wisdom.

— **Coleman Barks**
Noted translator of the works of Sufi poet Gelaluddin Rumi.

I have spent many hours being deeply touched and inspired by Paul Ferrini's words. Many people will receive beautiful gifts from them.

— **Judith Skutch Whitson**
President, Foundation for Inner Peace.

Paul Ferrini's wonderful books show a way to walk lightly with joy on planet earth!

— **Gerald Jampolsky, M.D.**
Author of *Love is Letting Go of Fear* and *Teach Only Love.*

"Paul Ferrini's writing is authentic, delightful and wise. It reconnects the reader to the Spirit Within, to that place where even our deepest wounds can be healed. "

—**Joan Borysenko, Ph.D.**
Author of *Guilt is the Teacher, Love is the Answer.*

Paul Ferrini brings a gentle synthesis of an awakening mind and an open heart. His writing points the way of the spiritual journey that we all share.

— **Alan Cohen**
Author of *The Dragon Doesn't Live Here Anymore*

Paul Ferrini's books lead us on a gentle journey to our true source of joy and happiness — inside our selves.

— **Ken Keyes, Jr.**
Author of *The Handbook to Higher Consciousness.*

What impresses me about Paul Ferrini's work is the lucid and poetic way he is able to express spiritual ideas. His writings are heartfelt and very valuable.

— **Stephen Schwartz**
Author of *The Compassionate Presence.*

Book Design by Elizabeth Lewis
Typesetting by Carolyn Meehan

Photography on pages 9,147 and 165 by Carol Foley
215 Mountain Home Park, Brattleboro, VT 05301

Photography on cover and pages 21,37,59
and 199 by Gene Parulis
RFD 2, Box 6, Brattleboro, VT 05301

Photography on pages 75,99,123 and 181 by Marc Caryl
P.O Box 3143, Taos, NM 87571

ISBN 1-879159-14-7

Manufactured in the United States of America

THE WISDOM OF THE SELF

Authentic Experience and the Journey to Wholeness

Paul Ferrini

Heartways Press
Santa Fe, New Mexico

Trust in the Self.
The Self in you
is the same Self in me.

Only when the Self
goes unrecognized
do conflicts arise.

You and I
are manifestations
of a Single Source
and share in its authority.

So long as we remember this,
how can there be a wound
too deep for healing,
or a sin that stands
beyond forgiveness' reach?

Trust in the Self.

Mistakes are blessings
that light the way
and help the dreamer
awaken from his dream.

Not one illusion stands
outside creation;
not a single fear eludes
love's embrace.

TABLE OF CONTENTS

INTRODUCTION • *Innocence and Experience*

INTRODUCTION

Innocence and Experience

"The healing and redemptive power of experience lies in its ability to access and give birth to the deepest part of ourselves."

———————•———————

Innocence and Experience

IT SEEMS A FOREGONE CONCLUSION that as we grow older, we become more skeptical and pessimistic about human nature. As Children, we are Innocent and Trusting. As we grow older, we are supposed to wise up. An adult who believes in the essential innocence of human beings is considered hopelessly naive and protected from the reality of life.

William Blake documented this growing pessimism about human nature in his *Songs of Innocence and Experience*. In the *Songs of Innocence* Blake charitably writes:

> *Mercy has a human heart,*
> *Pity, a human face:*
> *and Love the human form divine,*
> *and Peace the human dress.*

Later, in the Songs of Experience, he complains:

> *Cruelty has a human heart*
> *and Jealousy a human face*
> *Terror, the human form divine*
> *and Secrecy, the human dress.*

In Blake's experience, the lamb who is "meek and mild" becomes the tiger with his "fearful symmetry," and the Clod of Clay who says:

> *love seeketh not Itself to please*
> *nor for itself hath any care;*
> *but for another gives its ease,*

And builds a Heaven in Hell's despair.
becomes the Pebble of the Brook who proclaims:
> *love seeketh only Self to please,*
> *to bind another to Its delight:*
> *Joys in another's loss of ease,*
> *and builds a Hell in Heaven's despite.*

This then seems to be the way of experience, rubbing out our youthful hope, trust, and enthusiasm about life. Our time on earth does not increase our faith in ourselves or each other, not to mention our faith in the divine.

A Course in Miracles challenges this assumption and the whole litany of despair that goes with it. It tells us:
> *to see a guilty world is but the sign your*
> *learning has been guided by the world,*
> *and you behold it as you see yourself.*

Text 613

Our pessimism about the world is the mirror image of our indictment of ourselves. We have projected our despair and lack of self-acceptance outward onto others. We think it condemns them and not us, but that is merely our conceit. In truth, what we reject or condemn in others merely shows us what we cannot stomach in ourselves.

Given the intensity of our judgment of ourselves, it is not easy to affirm our lives. At best, we affirm certain aspects of our experience and deny or reject others. This sets up a dichotomy within consciousness. Part of me is acceptable and another part is not. This keeps my judgment of myself running at an unconscious level. It also continually fuels the mechanism of projection, since it is easier for me to direct my hatred at others than at myself.

The concept of evil or of original sin is kept alive in my partial rejection of myself and my projection of these unacceptable qualities onto my brother. Only in the acceptance of my wholeness or my brother's do I eschew the concept of sin. And only in my forgiveness of my mistakes and my brother's do I come to embrace the totality of my humanness or his.

My "rediscovery" of my essential innocence and my brother's is thus tied head and tail to the forgiveness process. Without forgiving myself and him for our mistakes, I cannot re-establish my innocence or his in my own eyes. To put it simply, without forgiveness, only guilt remains. The guilty must perforce perceive a guilty world.

It is naive to think that we can experience our lives here without witnessing this profound guilt we feel, no matter how deeply it is buried in our psyches, no matter how adept we are at projecting it upon others. Sooner or later, we realize, as Blake does, that something in this kingdom is amiss. We grow wary of the Pollyannas and Panglosses in our lives for we understand that all is not for "the best in this best of all possible worlds."

To put it simply, we begin to face our egos head on. We see the effects of the steady stream of judgments we make. We begin to look at our own darkness and to pay less attention to the blackness in our brother's eye.

That is the turning point. That is the point when we become really honest with ourselves, when we begin to learn to accept our whole experience, not just the part we find comforting. We stop being selective learners. We learn to look at what upsets us too. We understand that it is precisely this part of our experience which provides us with the greatest opportunity for growth. By engaging the forgiveness process here, where we are most raw and defensive, we mine the brightest gold. The Course tells us that the holiest spot on earth is where "an ancient hatred" is transformed into "a present love."

In the acceptance of the totality of our experience, our original innocence is born anew. This is not the innocence that comes from naiveté or lack of experience, nor is it the innocence that comes through denial of experience. It is innocence born of the acceptance of whatever life brings.

Here, Innocence and Experience are not at odds, as Blake proposes. Nor is experience synonymous with pessimism and lack of faith or hope. Indeed, experience—even the most terrible kinds—can give birth to a stronger faith. As Victor Frankl, Elie Weisel and other concentration camp survivors have pointed out, external indignities can sometimes forge an extraordinary inner strength. Former hostages such as Terry Waite and Terry Anderson have echoed these sentiments.

Life is our teacher. We can learn form whatever it brings us. To find the value in our experience does not mean to pretend that "bad things never happen." To deny our suffering is to refuse what it would teach us. The healing and redemptive power of experience lies in its ability to access and give birth to the deepest part of ourselves.

When our experience results in profound learning, we cannot classify it as good or bad. Rather, we learn to see it as a necessary part of our growth. That doesn't mean that we would want to repeat it. But we are thankful for the lessons it teaches us.

Pain is not always necessary, but to think that we can move through life without pain (resistance to psychological change), is wishful thinking. Each one of us experiences our fears and the psychological contractions that accompany them. This is part of the birthing process. We must see and confront our fear to move beyond it.

Because life brings each of us challenges does not mean that we lose our innocence. If we own the challenge and move through it, forgiving ourselves and others as we go, we actualize that innocence. However if we perceive the challenge as a punishment, we keep our artificial guilt alive and adopt the role of passive victim. Unfortunately, victims are incapable of learning, because they do not know how to take responsibility for their lives.

Learning from our experience does not mean rationalizing or justifying what happens. Often, we are completely baffled by the lessons that come our way. That is okay. We do not have to make these situations fit within our conceptual boundaries. Indeed, our lessons often come into our lives to disturb those boundaries. Our willingness to open ourselves to the teaching of our experience is enough to initiate the learning process.

The Journey of Self is cyclical. It moves from unconscious innocence to conscious guilt, from conscious guilt to forgiveness, and from forgiveness to conscious innocence. The journey's goal is not reached by overlooking, projecting, or denying our experience. It is reached through acceptance and scrutiny of the whole of what life brings to us moment to moment. The authentic journey does not avoid conflict, but teaches us to move through it, own it, and release it.

The journey of Self takes us through the development of the ego and its mechanism of separation. It shows us the suffering that results from the ego's fearful need to manipulate experience. And it helps us learn to walk through our fears, trusting in the wisdom of the universal Self within.

The first phase of this journey requires individuation, the acceptance of our unique experience in totality, regardless of the pressures brought to bear on us to conform to group norms or capitulate to outside authority. It is a journey from the inside out, from unconsciousness to consciousness. Its goal is authenticity. Its tool is separation.

The second phase of the journey involves unification or at-one-ment, the recognition that our own experience is not that different from the experience of others. And, in this recognition, we learn to emphasize that aspect of our experience which is "archetypal" or held in common with others. Whereas we emphasized what was different about our experience in the first phase, here we emphasize what is similar.

The urge to share and to communicate is born. The individual self (with a small "s") gives birth to the universal Self (with a capital "S"), and Christ is born on earth.

We begin this journey with a wholeness we do not consciously comprehend. It has a divine Source, but we do not recognize it as such. Our attention faces outward. We want to understand the world. We develop the ability to comprehend that which stands outside us by separating from other human beings and from our Source. Our ability "to know" depends on our standing apart, comparing, judging, observing.

We look for truth and happiness outside of ourselves, but we do not find it. At best, we find aborted relationships which disturb our peace and prompt us to look for the cause of our pain within our own consciousness. Now the observer becomes the observed. The spiritual path is initiated. We learn to look upon our own darkness and bring it to the light. We find devil and angel within and unite them into one complex, multifaceted being. The divided self has accepted its at-one-ment.

At the beginning of the journey our innocence was held unconsciously. Now we hold it in full awareness. We affirm ourselves without reservation. We accept our mistakes.

Having found the light within, we begin to see it in others. Our only goal becomes to be a messenger of love, to help others accept the at-one-ment for themselves. We are no longer intimidated by a world in which violence seems to prevail, for we understand this as but a symptom of the separated self. It is a heart-rending cry for love, one that we heard issue from our own lips when we looked at the source of our pain.

From our own journey, we know the veil of fear that hides the light. We do not need to deny the pain our sister feels. Yet we know that this veil can be lifted and Christ will come in answer to her call for help. We stand as a reminder of that answer, which has come to us, a silent witness to the divinity within us all.

The unification of Self represents not only the birth of Christ within, but His birth in the World. Having unified the dualities within consciousness, we no longer see a separation between self and other. Each being is the manifestation of the One Eternal Self that dwells within the heart of all beings.

Now does the lion lay down with the lamb, and so is original innocence strengthened in the fire of authentic experience. Our lessons are learned and we give thanks for them. For we are not victims of the world we see, but its busy architects. And now we understand the power that was given us for all time, the power to choose what we would be.

Now we return to God, healed and made whole, having rejected short cuts and false idols, having disclaimed the need for specialness, which creates division within and separates us from one another. Instead we choose equality, which permits joining and celebrates the simple beauty of the undivided Self.

Separation is a thing of the past, one phase on the journey home. Was it really necessary? Did it really occur? Or is it, like the journey itself, just a metaphor for our process of remembering who we are. Now we know without a doubt that there is just one Self, not two or three. And Christ is but the bridge from duality to oneness. He is not separate from God, nor are we.

A *Course in Miracles* tells us:

> *You will make many concepts of the self as learning goes along. Each one will show the changes in your own relationships, as your perception of yourself is changed . . . (Yet) There will come a time when images have all gone by, and you will see you know not what you are. It is to this unsealed and open mind that truth returns, unhindered and unbound. Where concepts of self have been laid by is truth revealed exactly as it is.* Text 613

There is but one truth shared by all. Yet each of us comes to it uniquely. Diversity is our gift to God. Unity is God's gift to us. When we are no longer afraid of our differences, they will cease to divide us. Unity within diversity is the sign that Christ has been born in our hearts and minds and in the holy places where we meet.

May we each affirm the uniqueness of our lives. May we embrace the good and the bad, high and low, laughter and tears. May we move through the fire with open eyes. There is nothing that is unworthy of us. There is no lesson that comes without a gentle reminder that we are loved and valued exactly as we are.

Owning Our Whole Experience

"Before we can return home as light bearers we must find the light in the darkness of our souls."

———•———

Owning Our Whole Experience

Gathering Light in the Dark Places

A MAN'S* BELIEFS must keep stride with his experiences. When he has been shielded from pain and grief, he can sing of the sky, but not of the earth. His mind stretches away from his heart, doing cartwheels of love in the thin air. His spirituality comes from the fairy realm.

But the skysongs of a man who has been touched by suffering and grief sound flat. He cannot sing them anymore. Their airy sound cannot lift the heavy veil that shrouds his soul after deep emotional challenge such as the death of a child, the onset of a serious illness, or the breakup of a longstanding relationship.

He must go into his grief, through his suffering. He must walk through his dark thoughts, his half cried tears. He must descend to the valley to bathe

---

* The use of the masculine singular pronoun seems appropriate here, since the myth that we wish to explode has flourished in a male-dominated, patriarchal culture. The new myth requires the integration of feminine values of sensitivity, pluralsim, and circularity, which we all need to learn.

his wounds before he can begin the long climb up the mountain. That is his path of grace.

He begins heavy with darkness, and ever so slowly lifts himself up the winding path through rain, mud and snow. He slips and slides, pulls himself forward, step by step. When he reaches the treeline, he pauses in silence. He knows he has paid for his climb with callouses on the feet and scrapes on his face. Yet the first views from that promontory of stone looking down over the town and lake below make it all worthwhile.

After a man has climbed his first mountain, he is no longer naive about either the descent or the climb. His body knows well what it will be required to do. There are no illusions any more. A weak man stops here, and declines to ascend a second time. When troubles come, he hides from them. He neither descends into his grief nor ascends to his joy. He becomes frozen in time, like a man in a three piece suit trapped in an elevator on the 32nd floor.

But a strong man descends whenever his life tells him he must. He goes down to the lake to shed his tears and he climbs to his craggy perch among the clouds. Each time, there are new surprises, new demands. Each time, his heart is strengthened and his mind opened. That is the nature of the journey.

There is a longstanding myth that says the climb is strictly a vertical one. Every lesson learned represents some measure of progress on the climb to the top. Those who reach the top become enlightened. Those who don't, come back in different bodies and begin the climb again.

This myth says that holy men stay at the top. True, the Buddha may climb back down to help other sentient beings or Christ may be born in a manger, but the journey for most of us is still seen as a one-time, upward journey. Darkness is not acknowledged except as a place to escape from. Its power to birth the man is not recognized.

This myth denies the interrelated power of darkness and of light within the heart of every being. In this myth, darkness is vanquished by light. The myth is linear, presumptuous, hierarchical and moralistic. It does not speak to our times.

A new myth is now forming. In this myth life is an up and down journey we take many times. Enlightenment is not a single event that happens only at the top. It is a continual event that happens as much in the shadows as it does in the vistas. Man's soul is the container of the journey. The directions up and down are just symbolic of the fact that both heaven and hell are found within consciousness.

In the new myth, joy arises out of the embrace of sadness. Love emerges out of the confrontation with fear. Light is found in the darkness and brought forth. At first, it may be a tiny spark, barely visible in the dark folds of mind. Nourished and protected deep within, this tiny spark lights a single candle, and the candle illuminates the altar.

Light begins in each heart in this way. In each heart it is expanded and offered out to others, or folded back within. In each heart, it is strengthened by friendship, tested by grief, and confounded by selfishness and greed.

It doesn't work to try to make the dual world singular by denying either darkness or light. The only way to reconcile differences is to embrace both sides at the same time. That is what spirituality is for a man who lives on earth. He must own both gods and devils or he does not give birth to his true self.

Society has taught us to hide our sins and disguise our weaknesses. If we do that, we will not bring them to the light. They will remain in the shadows of the mind and the light of forgiveness will be shrouded in guilt.

Let us proclaim our sins. That is the true Christian teaching. The ritual of confession should not be a one-way game played with priest behind a curtain. It must be a two-way process to be effective. The early Christians knew this. Their gatherings created a sacred space in which people felt safe sharing their guilt and their shame. By sharing it, they did not hold onto it.

One person did not sit back in judgment. Everyone participated.

Anyone can play the authentic role of the priest by listening without judgment. That is what co-counseling is about. In co-counseling, both priest and parishioner get to confess and be forgiven. It is a mutual experience. That way, neither person gets caught in the roles. Both speak. And both listen.

Mutuality and equality are essential ingredients of the new myth.

Ours is not a solitary journey, but a shared one. What we do for ourselves and what we do for others are one and the same. Each gesture reflects the other.

The new myth says spirituality is a daily, hourly, moment by moment affair. If I yell at my kids and then go meditate, I must own both acts. My spirituality is the awareness I bring to all of my life. I cannot separate out one day of the week and make it holy. I can't be holy in one part of my life and degrading in another. I am the whole of what I think, the whole of what I act.

The old myth wants to divide life into two distinct parts: high and low, good and bad, me and you. It wants to separate our spirituality from the rest of our lives. That creates a false spirituality. It creates a dogma, a catechism, a product that can be marketed. But it does not create a living spirituality.

A spirituality that lives and moves and breathes goes backwards and forwards, up and down, and all around. It completely embraces our lives. In it God is not afraid to shake hands with Satan. Why would S/he be? A living God moves through duality and fear in order to move beyond them.

If I have to deny any aspect of who I am to be spiritual then I am creating an illusionary spirituality. My spirituality must jive with who I am or it is not authentic. If my God does not live and move and breathe, like I do, then it is a one-dimensional creation of my own fear and denial.

It is time to grow up. We need to stop putting God above us where we can never measure up. And we need to stop putting ourselves above God where we get in over our heads. We can stand face to face with God without denying our power or His.

God lives in me when I can accept myself

completely as I am, with all my darkness, all my sins, all my weaknesses. And I dwell in God when I accept my life exactly as it is, with all its problems and conflicts. This is the synergistic stance of a man who embraces life even as he learns from it.

A man who refuses to learn denies himself and others. He builds a prison around where he stands. He keeps himself locked in, separated from others, or inappropriately dependent on them for the release he must give himself.

God will not come to meet us so long as we insist on this charade. He does not take his stand along side us until we free ourselves from imagined wounds. So long as we blame Him or each other, we cannot meet Him.

Only when we stand forth in self-affirmation without blame or shame do we stand with God. And only in such moments can we truly meet, for then His will and ours cease to be at odds.

Discovering
Inner Authority

M EN AND WOMEN try to interpret God to one another, but it never works. God does not need an intermediary. Even Christ is not an intermediary, for Christ is within each of us.

Christ is my perfection and yours, my innocence and yours, my unconditional love and acceptance and yours. Jesus was a man who knew the Christ within. He was a shining example, but he was not alone. The Christ consciousness is available to all of us. We already live in Christ and do not know it.

So how can I presume to tell you what God is or what God wants for you. Sure, I can say that God is love and that God wants you to love. But, beyond that, I can't really say. Beyond that I'm trespassing on your own sacred space.

Anyone who would prescribe for another had better learn what he would preach for himself. The need to prescribe for others shows weakness and scarcity within. One who is happy does not presume to tell others how to be happy. He simply radiates his happiness. He witnesses. His words and deeds do not say different things.

The lessons of inner authority have been hard for us to learn. We threw off the cloak of organized religion only to find ourselves bowing down before gurus. The idea that the guru knows better than we do what's best for us is another form of slavery. Christ does not ask for slaves, but for free men.

Sure, it is tempting to become a guru, and just as tempting to serve one. Both are gestures in which I deny responsibility for my life. If I am to come to truth deeply, I must understand that there is never a time when I am not responsible for myself. I can deny my life by becoming responsible for yours. Or I can deny my life by letting you become responsible for it. These are ego gestures. They punctuate the world of push-pull, of attack and guilt.

I think I am being nice to you by taking the responsibility from your shoulders, but this is attack. This is invasion. The fact that you give me permission does not change the reality of the transgression for each of us.

I cannot live my life through you. That is the great seduction, that you have something that I don't have, or vice-versa, that I must follow you or you must follow me.

If I need you to follow me, I am a coward. Let me learn to stand alone.

A brave woman moves from the inside out. She dances to the song of her heart. She does not want a mate who mimics her, but one whose song enriches hers.

Joinings out of weakness bring disappointment, for they are false at the start. It is no wonder they fall apart. This kind of hurt can be avoided if we strengthen ourselves before joining others.

Real joining is a sign of strength and abundance. It is a celebration. Our joy brings us together.

Inner authority is difficult for all of us to cultivate, yet it is the cornerstone of our spiritual growth. We cannot grow if we do not take responsibility for our own lives. We can't grow as long as we are concerned with what others are doing. We can't grow so long as our focus is on changing the world.

Each person is alone before God. That recognition comes in a moment of trembling. There is no one who bids me approach or turn away. That is my choice. There has never been a time when that choice did not belong to me.

Yet my nakedness before God does not make me special. Hearing the word of God in my life simply allows me to take my rightful place in His plan. Everyone must do this sooner or later.

To help another, I must encourage her to trust and believe in herself. I must encourage her to trust and believe in the goodness of others. I must encourage her to trust and believe in the unconditional goodness of God.

That is how I help. That is how I speak the word of God. Anything else is just small talk. It is better left unsaid.

If I do not have something positive to say to you, I cannot have a good influence on you. To speak positively to you, I must speak positively to myself.

Let me be honest. What is the nature of my internal dialogue? Are my thoughts loving and helpful?

Am I loving myself right now? Am I loving you right now? Am I empowering you and myself?

Any judgment I make about myself or you brings dark clouds into my mind. Any feelings of guilt encase my mind in steel. Futility, disappointment, despair tie the unconditional world down, making it behave as my thoughts dictate.

Who is in charge here?

You see, the responsibility will not go away.

We wonder why so many multi-millionaire, "holier than thou" preachers have a secret fondness for prostitutes or young boys. We wonder why so many gurus preaching non-attachment spend much of their waking hours trying to get their female disciples into bed. I say, thank God for these lessons.

No one else has the answer. No one else is more together. No one else has knowledge that you do not have. Whatever is in Lao Tzu, or Buddha, or Jesus is in you. A real guru tells you that.

Shri Nisargadatta would tell the people who came to listen to him. "Okay, now you have heard. Go away. You don't need me anymore."

The real teacher is within. Outer teachers are helpful, but we must be careful not to get attached to them. It isn't good for them and it isn't good for us.

If a teaching resonates, take it into your heart. Learn it and live it from there. Practice it day by day, moment by moment. That's real spiritual practice. That is commitment to the teacher within.

Overcoming
Our Victimhood

W E ALL ENTER this world with some sense of inadequacy about who we are. Our self-doubt attracts us toward relationships in which that doubt can be made conscious and explicit.

Victims of violence and sexual abuse understandably have difficulty taking responsibility for their collaboration in these events. That is why it is important to be explicit in pinpointing just where responsibility lies, and where it does not.

Clearly it does not lie in the realm of conscious choice. A child does not ask to be sexually abused or beaten. Any attempt to make the child responsible in this respect is an attack against the dignity of the child.

Yet, at a deeper level, the child must own the experience because it happened to him. He may feel guilty about it. He may feel angry about it. And he must work through these feelings, whatever they are.

Eventually, if he is to heal, he must come to a place where he realizes that he is not stained by the experience, that in a sense he is stronger than the experience. It is paradoxical. He feels like a victim, but the only way he can survive the experience is to refuse to allow himself to be a victim. So he rises up and uses his experience to help others. He finds a way to empower himself and to empower others.

And so his experience of abuse becomes a means for healing a deep sense of inadequacy which he brought with him into this embodiment. The same thing happens to the perpetrator. His unprovoked attack against others forces him to see and deal with his deep-seated self-hatred.

Whatever hidden beliefs or assumptions we have about ourselves will be externalized in some way in our relationships. Everything that happens outside of us reflects an inner state.

That does not mean that we consciously create our suffering! But it does mean that our unconscious creations are being brought to the light so that we can examine them and their effects. We are asked to look at the causes of our suffering so that we can choose whether we are willing to pay the price.

Every instance of abuse is an opportunity for healing for both perpetrator and victim. By insisting that one person is innocent and the other guilty, we deny the possibility for healing. As such, we prevent ourselves from discovering the original, albeit unconscious, motivation for the event, which is shared in some manner by both parties.

Of course, perpetrator and victim do not have to become friends for healing to take place. But each must understand what brought him or her to that event. And each must learn from it a lesson that affirms and empowers.

If we are honest, we realize that every one of us

has been a perpetrator at some time in our lives. And every one of us has been a victim. Indeed, it's well documented that victims become perpetrators, and we're just beginning to understand how perpetrators become victims.

To think that any of us can come into this life and not experience some kind of abuse is not only naive, it is the worst kind of denial. We are here in this embodiment to become conscious of our trespasses against others, as well as theirs against us. Gradually, after many instances of push-pull, we begin to see and address the inner dynamic behind our repetitive experience. Slowly we identify the beliefs in our minds that lead us into the fray.

So abuse is a pathway to equality. It sounds macabre, but it's true. Abusing or being abused heightens one's awareness of equality. It's an incredible lesson if we're willing to learn it. If not, it just keeps getting more intense until we do.

Let us be clear. Our understanding of abuse does not justify it. Those who abuse others must pay the price. That is how they learn. What is important is not that they are punished for their mistakes, but that they learn from them.

Don't forget, many people are punished for their mistakes but don't learn from them. Their punishment merely confirms their belief that they are not worthy of acceptance and love. That increases their sense of separation and aggravates their tendency to attack back.

Learning and forgiveness go hand in hand. Yet who can offer forgiveness? Only one who has faced the darkness inside himself can turn to a murderer and see the light of God in his eyes.

Until we embrace our own darkness, it will be impossible for us to understand the trespasses of others, never mind forgive them. We always hold others to a higher standard than the one to which we hold ourselves. That is the basis of our continued attack against each other.

Abuse can only be ended when we accept a single standard for ourselves and others. In truth, there is only one standard. For as we treat others, so we treat ourselves. That is the law. It is only our self-deception which would have us believe that we can be terrible to others and nice to ourselves or terrible to ourselves and nice to others. The sadist and masochist both violate the law of equality.

PART TWO
·

The Self as the
Primary Metaphor

"The Self is not a known territory, but a wilderness. Too often we forget that. Too often we reach the boundaries of what we know about ourselves and turn back."

———— • ————

The Self as the Primary Metaphor

Knowledge
of Self

T HE KNOWLEDGE OF SELF is and must be grounded in the experience of Self. Beneath all our woundedness, all our incompleteness, there is a shining being, innocent and free, a being so bright it burns away all the shadows, all the fears.

This being of light is our true nature. We sense it, but do not believe in it fully. We are awakening to it. We are exploring the possibility that it exists. We have a preliminary experience and, as such, a tentative knowledge.

It is not a deep knowledge. For a deep knowledge is based on a deep experience. And a deep knowledge brings with it a certainty that we do not yet have.

We needn't feel bad about where we are. It is, in truth, a beautiful place. We are awakening to our true nature. We are coming to know who we really are.

And, in the process, we are having to discard a lot of ideas about ourselves, about others, and about the nature of reality. As we awaken, we surrender more and more beliefs.

As we discard our mistaken beliefs, the truth about us shines forth with clarity and intensity. The dark clouds give way to a perpetual sun. We see our own steadiness and strength. We see that we are not dependent on anyone else for sustenance. We are the Source.

As each one of us awakens to this fact, he realizes that all he sought for outside himself exists in the Self, perpetually, and without conditions. It is simply up to him to see this.

This wounded child inside that hungers for love does not know that she is the Christ. She feels incomplete, but there is nothing incomplete about her. She feels abused, broken, rejected, but she sits unknowingly alongside the angels.

In the healing process the ego, the wounded one, the guilty one, comes to understand that it creates its own misery. It stops projecting responsibility for its pain onto others. It sits with its pain and asks for help. It agrees to listen and be quiet. It invites the Self to come forward.

And the Self comes like a deep wave, and ego is enfolded in this wave like a tiny river merging into a mighty one. Joining with the bringer of love, ego learns to bring love to itself.

The great judge, the bringer of shame and blame, learns to bring love. It learns to accept itself exactly as it is. It learns to be without judgment in a single instant. And in that instant, all of the shame is washed away. And the child knows that she is loved.

And in that instant Christ is born within.

Being the Self means recognizing that same Self in others. You cannot be the Self and not recognize the Self in others because it is the same Self.

Yet unless you become the Self, you cannot see It in others. Only the Self sees the Self. Ego cannot see the Self. But when ego ceases to judge, when it ceases to attack, it invites the Self forward. And then it begins to bless itself, and to bless others, and true in-sight returns.

The Self is the primary metaphor. Even the metaphor of "the wounded child" is part of the metaphor of the Self. If you say that the child is innocent, then you are talking about the Self. If you believe that wounds can be healed, then you are talking about the Self.

Only if you say that the child is guilty are you using a different metaphor. That is the metaphor of "original sin," which is based on the belief that the separation from God is real. This metaphor says some part of the body of Christ can be diseased, condemned, cut off from the whole. If that is the truth, then there can be no redemption.

If there is salvation for one person, but not for another, if there is salvation for one who accepts Jesus, but not for one who does not, then salvation itself is conditional. How can that which "restores" us to the Body of Christ be conditional? It just is not possible.

Only unconditional love restores, for only unconditional love refuses to accept the concept of original brokenness. We may be wounded in time, but we are not wounded in eternity. The wound itself is a learning experience, a process, a rite of passage.

We do not seek to deny "wounding" as a process in the growth of consciousness. But we do deny that it has any existential value. One is not worthy or unworthy because one is wounded. Indeed, the wound teaches that healing is possible. And healing teaches that the wound was never real.

But to say that the wound is not real before healing has happened is not helpful. One must acknowledge and experience the wound. The wound is a teaching about forgiveness, both to the one who gave the wound and the one who received it. The wound is a lesson.

The knowledge of Self is impossible without the experience of Self, and the experience of Self requires the experience of all that is not-Self. What is not-Self gives the wound. It must be recognized. Ego must be seen for what it is.

Yet one must not hate ego. Hating the ego just keeps one from experiencing love. You can't experience love by hating yourself or hating others. Hating the wound-giver does not help the wound heal, nor does hating oneself for being a victim.

All that is not-Self still belongs to Self in some way. It's hard to wake up to self-abuse without having the mirror that our push-pull relationships provide.

So part of the Self becomes victim or it becomes perpetrator to bring to consciousness a deeply-felt inadequacy. That part of the Self is not bad. It is a teacher and a great actor. It convinces us that it is real. It personifies the error so that we can see it. But it is not the error.

What seems to separate from Self (call it ego) is never really separate. It simply goes out to come back. It personifies beliefs that must be let go. And as they are let go, it returns to its Source.

Every moment, Self is becoming not-Self so that we can see what is not true, and every time we see what is not true we return to what is true. This is the dance we all do. There is nothing evil about it.

We are all witnessing error, not to make it real, but to uncover our belief in it. We need to see our guilt before we can let it go. We need to understand that all our feelings of separation come from our belief in the old myth of "original sin."

We all made the error real. We must see how this manifests in our lives. We must look at the not-Self to return to the Self.

Only the Self is real. Even the not-Self belongs to the Self. Even ego is contained in Self. Even evil is contained in the goodness of God.

Ego cannot taint Self. Evil cannot corrupt the Good. For Self will accept no opposite. And Good never ceases to be Good even when evil is practiced.

Good and evil are not on the same footing. Goodness is real. Evil is the apparent absence of goodness. But how can something that is true existentially cease to exist. How can goodness become absent? It is not possible! Goodness is everpresent. Only the perception of goodness ebbs and flows.

So evil is a function of perception. But Goodness is not. Ego is a function of perception, but Self is not. Perception exists inside of knowledge, but it is not the same as knowledge.

Perception is always partial. Knowledge is always whole. Ego is always partial. Self is always whole.

Perception can merge with knowledge by surrendering. Ego can merge with Self by surrendering. The feeling of absence can be healed by surrendering to the abundance of the moment. Scarcity cannot exist where there is gratitude.

So perception leads to various states of consciousness that are limited. That is inevitable. But Being is not limited. It cannot be limited.

Being is whole and self-sustaining. It is goodness without opposition, without guilt or the belief in sin.

Self is existential. Each Self is a manifestation of Unlimited Being. It does not change in its value. It is always Good.

Ego is situational and conditional. It is based on perception and judgment. It changes as situations change. It changes as beliefs change.

Yet even ego, as far away as it seems from the realm of pure Being, belongs to it. It could not exist apart from Being. Life of any kind, regardless of how limited, could not be possible without unlimited Being.

Of each manifest being, all you can truly say is that it belongs to the unmanifest One. Whatever seems to be distinct or different is just the nature of this play, this journey of consciousness.

Each manifest being is awakening to its

unmanifest Source. It creates a manifest world to learn that its power does not lie outside of itself. It creates a world of struggle and pain to understand that peace is its eternal possession. It dreams that it may awaken from the dream. It separates from Its Source so that it can realize that it is free to come and go, and that, no matter how far it strays, it is never too far way to find its way home.

That is the Journey of Self, which *A Course in Miracles* calls "a journey without distance to a goal that has not changed." It is a journey of consciousness awakening to its own innocence, its own power and beauty.

The Self is omniscient, omnipresent, and omnipotent. To it belongs all that can be seen, felt, or understood. Every one of us abides in the embrace of Self. That is all we know and all that we will ever need to know.

The knowledge of Self and the experience of Self are one and the same. You cannot have one without the other.

Remembering Self

SELF IS THE UNCONDITIONAL SOURCE of love and well-being. When we don't feel loved or loving, we are not in touch with Self. We don't cease being the Self in those moments. We just cease being aware of the Self. In that sense, we are never cut-off from our Source, but we think that we are. We feel that we are.

All that changes in moving from misery to joy is our awareness. External conditions rarely change so quickly. But consciousness can change in a flash. It simply requires a moment of acceptance.

All that is necessary for my own healing is a change in consciousness. All that is necessary for the healing of the planet is a change in consciousness. Such a change in the mind-set of an individual or a species will eventually usher in a corresponding change in physical conditions. But if we try to change the conditions without changing the consciousness behind them, our efforts are doomed to failure.

To heal, to restore joy and peace within, each person must become responsible for her own consciousness. Each thought that she thinks, every emotion that she feels creates the contents of consciousness. Negative thoughts and emotions create a consciousness obsessed with struggle and difficulty, a consciousness in which everyone is crucified by the mistake she makes. Positive thoughts and emotions create a consciousness characterized by flexibility and forgiveness, in which mistakes can be made and learned from.

A consciousness filled with negative thoughts and emotions is always inadequate, jealous, competitive, and greedy. That is because it cannot remember its connection to its Source. It seeks reinforcement in the world. Of course, this never works.

If you want to get reinforcement, the world is not a very good place to look. This is not because the world is "evil" or even because people are "evil." It is because the collective consciousness tends to be negative in nature. Just look at the stories on television and in the newspapers. They personify our worst fears.

On some level, the world exists to reflect whatever is in consciousness. Our fear produces a mad, violent, impatient world, a world where other people are seen as objects, not as subjects.

This is why love cannot move into the world unless it is carried by the consciousness of one who is positive, optimistic and trusting. People who become channels for love join together and model a different world. That is what is beginning to happen now.

Obviously, this is being done in the nick of time. Just when the planet is about to swallowed up by the collective negativity, a movement toward the light begins in the hearts and minds of individuals.

Slowly it spreads to small groups. Spiritual families form, and from them communities evolve. It does not happen all at once. It is a gradual process, based on choices made by hundreds and thousands of individuals.

So each one of us is responsible for what we think and feel. We choose what our minds will focus on. We bless or we condemn. We attack or we forgive.

It is really no more complicated than this. Every choice produces a result in consciousness and in experience.

If I do not feel loved or loving, I attack. My attack simply demonstrates my feelings of inadequacy. Then I feel guilty for attacking, which reinforces my inadequacy and increases my likelihood to attack again. This is how most of us live most of the time.

We have forgotten the Self in ourselves and others. We have taken our wounds too seriously. The hurt child stands up inside our soul and says "don't forget about me. All this spirituality is nice, but it doesn't put food on the table. It doesn't guarantee me the recognition I want."

Darkness comes back in. But that's okay. We mustn't panic. Everything that feels injured must be healed. Every negative thought or emotion must be brought to the light.

It doesn't happen all at once. It happens as we are ready.

Remembering Self is a process. Ramana Maharshi taught his disciples to ask "Who is this one who thinks, or moves, or responds? Who is this?"

Is this the wounded child who feels cut off from his Source or the Self that is united with its Source? In every moment, we need to ask this question. Is this the one who loves or the one who feels unloved? Is this the one who fears, or the one who walks through his fears?

Can you think of a better question to ask? It brings us right to the answer.

If I have to ask, then it is probably the one who does not know. It is probably the wounded one, the one who struggles and feels confused. But that's okay, because he has an ally now. The power of mind is focused on him. Consciousness enters his cry of pain. By bringing awareness to the wound, we help to heal it.

So the answer is not just "this is the wounded one who speaks," but "this is the wounded one who is healing." Both the question and the answer are together.

Before the question was asked, the pain was unconscious. But now that the question is asked clearly, the pain can be felt and communicated. Now the child's cry for love can be heard.

Who is this who responds? It is none other than the one crying out for love! He knows that he needs love. And so he is able to receive it.

Let us not underestimate this knowledge. We find the Self by healing our brokenness. We find the Self by increasing our awareness of all the darkness in our minds. Awareness itself is the light with which we see.

In the light of awareness, nothing is ugly, nothing

is shameful, nothing is incapable of being redeemed. In the light of awareness, judgments cannot stand for long. Guilt fizzles. Anger is diffused.

Awareness does not fix the problem, but shows it to us clearly. Once we see it, we know it has a simple solution. For behind any problem stands a perceived lack of love. Restore the perception of love, of care, of kindness, and the problem can be seen differently.

A Course in Miracles talks in great depth about this crucial change in perception. It is the essential aspect of the miracle itself. But where does this change come from?

If you change your mind when you feel inadequate and cut off, you can connect with the Source of love. But what if you can't change your mind without connecting first to the Source?

Which comes first: the chicken or the egg?

It seems to me that changing our minds has a lot to do with accepting ourselves unconditionally and working through our feelings. If we can do that, we can change our minds.

If we can't, our mind-set remains the same.

Healing and integration happen through acceptance, not through rejection. To reject the ego is not to heal. To reject the brokenness, the cry for love, is to perpetuate the wound.

The Self contains everything, dark and light, woundedness and wholeness. If woundedness cannot be contained within wholeness, then it is not wholeness. If the cry for love cannot be contained within Self, then it is not Self.

Self is larger than anything that would restrict or oppose it. It is not at odds with anything internal or external. It is not a bundle of actions or conditions, but an unconditional state of being that exists in all of us.

To know the Self is to allow everything, to embrace the totality of who were are, all that we think and feel, all of our fear, all of our love. Our problems come when we draw a line and say: "Everything up to this line is okay with me. But everything on the other side I just can't accept." Every time I draw a line, I create artificial boundaries which prevent me from feeling joy and peace in my life.

Pointing out my fear won't help me erase the line. I will feel judged and extend the line. If you see my fear, please don't point it out to me. That just makes me more fearful. When you see my fear, find a way to love me. Then you are a true brother or sister.

Then you make me right, not in what I do, but in who I am. You recall me to the Self.

To recall me to the Self, you too must stand in the Self. To offer me love, you must offer it to yourself. To empower me, you must empower yourself.

Point out my weaknesses and illusions and you claim them for yourself. Remind me of my innocence and you confirm your own!

Accepting me is just an extension of your spiritual practice of accepting yourself. It is a mirror image of that practice. It lets you know how you are doing and what you still need to work on. Your acceptance of me is a barometer of your acceptance of yourself.

Remember, there are not two Selves, but only one. The Self in me is the same as the Self in you. If this were not true, there would be no equality, no communion, no grace.

If I would remember the Self in me, I must also remember it in you. This is not an isolated practice that leads me to a mountaintop. It is a daily, hourly, moment to moment practice that goes on through the ebb and flow of my life, through my relationships and my aloneness.

I do not have to change my life to embark on a spiritual practice. Indeed, if I need to change my life, I missed the most important ingredient of the practice.

I don't need to change your life either. If I need to change your life, it just means I'm afraid to take responsibility for healing my own perceptions. It just means that I'm not ready to begin.

When I'm ready, I just start. I don't look to you. I don't look for special conditions. I begin in this moment, with whatever conditions exist, with whatever relationships are present.

That is enough. The rest takes care of itself!

From Projection to Empowerment

WHEN I FEEL INADEQUATE, I think that I need to be better than you. My competitive behavior arises from something I feel within. Addressing that behavior does not help me change. To change, I must address its cause.

In this moment, I feel slighted, I feel that you do not recognize me. This is the truth, yet I cannot tell you this. I cannot be honest with you, because to be honest would mean admitting my feelings of inferiority and I believe that this would give you power over me.

So I puff myself up and come back at you self-important, combative, judgmental. I try to pay you back for not acknowledging me. This is the direct emotional experience. This is the naked event without justification.

I am afraid you are making a judgment of me, but I'm also afraid to check it out. I'm afraid to ask you "Are you judging me?" because, if the answer is yes, it will confirm my fears and, if the answer is no, I'll look like a fool. This is a no-win situation. My hands are tied. I am a prisoner of my own perceptions. And I remain a prisoner, even if my perceptions are totally unfounded.

To escape my prison, I must allow my perceptions to be questioned. When I think that you're judging me, I must be willing to check it out with you. Checking it out is an act of empowerment.

All communication is really about checking things out: "I thought you said this, but now I see that's not what you meant." Perhaps you didn't say what you meant. Perhaps I didn't hear what you said. It doesn't really matter who caused the confusion. Probably it was both of us. That's usually the case.

Do I need to make you wrong to come to the truth, or vice versa? If we both own the confusion, then we can both own the desire to come to clarity.

The past isn't over until we both own it. As long as we are disputing who was responsible for what, we haven't taken responsibility for what happened. So it is going to keep happening in our minds. The tape will keep running with all of our distorted perceptions playing over and over again.

When we're trying to assign blame, we're holding onto the past. We're holding onto the hurt. We're keeping the wound open to punish ourselves and others.

Communication is about taking responsibility for the past so that we can come to an understanding of present intention. "When you acted that way, I felt hurt. I felt judged. Now I realize that you were striking out at me because you felt the same way. You felt hurt too. I understand now that we both lost it. And I want you to know that it is not my intention to wound you."

Communication between us starts when we acknowledge our feelings. The child within will not dissociate from our adult persona so long as we honor our feelings. But if we try to cover over how we feel, if we deny or pretend, then watch out. This is where schizophrenia begins. When I deny my feelings, I dishonor my wholeness.

I must honor my feelings and be willing to share them with you, not because they are always "right," but because this is the primary gesture of trust and intimacy. Whether my feelings are right or your feelings are right isn't the issue. The issue is that we are willing to take the risk of sharing our woundedness.

When I can share my woundedness with you consciously, I decrease the likelihood that it will operate at an unconscious level in our relationship. It means dealing with a lot of feelings, some of which are exaggerated. There will be false alarms. But there will also be alarms that sound just as the fire is about to break out.

The movement from inferiority to superiority is arrested when our feelings of inferiority are acknowledged. Until they are acknowledged, they cannot be challenged. Unacknowledged, they slip into the unconscious, surfacing in our lives whenever they are triggered, often by seemingly unrelated events. Acknowledged, they provide us with a process of challenging our false ideas and beliefs about ourselves.

The need to project our inadequacy onto others falls away when we become willing to face it consciously. That means experiencing our deep-seated shame and guilt. It means experiencing our anger.

It is a difficult process, but it is a genuine act of self-liberation.

Communication, communion, community, all support this process. They represent the willingness of individuals to share their healing process. They reverse the tendency we all have to keep our feelings hidden, to remain isolated and alone with our anger or our shame.

We did not learn to feel inadequate all by ourselves. We learned to feel this way in a context in which others were learning the same mistaken lessons and all the defense mechanisms which go with them. So it is not surprising that we eventually find that others who are seeking to unlearn these beliefs can be helpful to us.

At first that may not be the case. But gradually, as we come to grips with our feelings of inadequacy and realize that others have similar feelings, we realize that interaction can help us. And we begin to see every instance of communication, communion, or community as an opportunity for continued growth.

In spite of the apparent differences between us, your pain and mine are not really very different. Your sadness, your feelings of isolation, your guilt, anger, and shame don't look that different from my own. We are all struggling with the same material. We learn in different ways at different times, but the lessons are quite similar.

As *A Course in Miracles* points out, the curriculum varies for each of us, but the experience of surrender is the same. When you find your peace, it doesn't matter how you got there. The tools that worked for you might work for someone else, or they might not. So you encourage everyone to discover their own tools, their own path to peace.

What more can you do? You can lead a friend to water, but you can't make him drink. Sometimes it is better to let him find the oasis himself. Then, he knows it is meant for him.

Each person will have the experience she needs when she is ready.

My witness may help her find her way or it may not. I do not always know when I am being helpful or when I am being helped. All I can do is try to accept what is offered and try to give what is needed. That's the best I can do. And that's always enough.

What isn't done through me will be done through someone else. And what doesn't come to me through you will come in another way, if it is what I really need.

PART THREE

Getting Out of Our Own Way

"The way to grace
is through surrender.
When I need to be in
control, the grace of
God cannot operate
with me and
through me."

———————•———————

Getting Out of Our Own Way

Not Needing
to Protect Others

NOT LONG AGO I helped organize a conference for students of *A Course in Miracles*. The Conference was an experience with lots of lessons and lots of confirmations. It began as a joining between two people who decided to say yes to each other. And it grew. One yes led to another yes and in just a few hours a whole conference was born.

Of course, we started with a certain level of enablement. We knew that people could take responsibility for their own accommodations. We would just provide the space and a group of workshops. We trusted the workshop leaders to share what they could.

There was one important exception, which turned out to provide me with a major lesson. One of the workshop leaders tended to be authoritarian in his approach to *A Course in Miracles*. I began to have second thoughts about his participation. I was afraid that he would sit there and read from the book and make pronouncements about The Course, exactly the approach I liked least and wanted to avoid in this conference.

Wouldn't you know it? There had to be some personification of my fear for me to work through! I agonized over this situation, and then finally let it go. Yet, still, I felt sorry for the people who had signed up for this workshop.

When the conference began, I was so busy, I forgot all about this workshop. Gradually, however, word about what happened reached me. My friend had done just what I thought he would do. Some of the participants were offended and walked out. Others tried to steer the workshop in a more participatory direction. But my friend went back to reading the book and making more pronouncements. He just couldn't hear what was being said to him.

Finally, the participants were so exasperated, they just took control of the workshop. They refused to let my friend read from the book. They insisted that they had come to share their experiences and that was what they were going to do! In the process, the workshop was transformed. It became a valuable experience for everyone. My friend got an important lesson about control, which he acknowledged, and the participants who stayed received a strong confirmation for taking responsibility for getting their needs met.

Instead of this workshop being one of the worst, as I feared, it became one of the best. It became a living lesson in authentic empowerment. It became a demonstration of how to take responsibility for self without attacking others.

Had I allowed my fear to intervene, I would have prevented an important event from happening. By trying to protect people from my friend's authoritarian approach, I would have become an authority myself. My friend would not have had his lesson and the conference participants would not have had theirs. I would have retained my lesson, but it might have come to me in a less charitable way. By allowing Spirit to be in control, my lesson was a gentle one. I saw the beauty of what happens when I get out of the way.

The way to grace is through surrender. When I need to be in control, the grace of God cannot operate with me and through me. The more I obsess about a certain situation, insisting that it be a certain way, the more I create complications and controversy.

When what I want isn't happening, I have a choice. I can accept what is happening and let go of what I want, or I can reject what is happening and insist on what I want. I have plenty of experience choosing the latter alternative, and it has never led either to abundance or to peace. I am learning, albeit slowly, to take a chance on the first alternative.

For example, during the conference, I was approached by my friend Jim. He was concerned that the way we had the chairs arranged in the workshop rooms was not ideal. He wanted to move them around so that they were grouped in a different way. At first I thought "Why is Jim making this so complicated? The chairs are fine the way they are." After some discussion, however, it became clear that Jim was not going to go away until he got my agreement about moving the chairs. Finally, when Jim offered to put the chairs back as he found them, I said "great. Do whatever you want to do."

Of course, I still felt this was a futile move, an example of ego getting involved and making everything more complicated. Strangely enough though, Jim's re-arrangement of the chairs worked just fine. The problems I thought would result were minor ones and there were some advantages I hadn't anticipated.

Would the other arrangement of chairs have worked as well? Probably. But that is a moot point. The key to this interaction seems to be this: My brother comes up to me and says he's not comfortable with something. He makes a suggestion about what he can do to make himself (and others, he believes) more comfortable. Moreover, he is willing to take responsibility for what he wants to do. How do you say no? It just isn't possible.

The truth is that it doesn't matter which way the chairs are set up. They are going to be moved anyway. The chairs never stay in the same place. Nothing in our lives remains the same. My role in life is not to insure that the chairs stay in a certain place.

But my role is to help my brother be as comfortable as he can be.

When I trust him, and his atonement, I see that it leads to good things.

Clearly, not trusting my brother leads to a contraction of energy and mires life in needless controversy. So, Jim, thank you for that lesson!

More and more I begin to realize that all God asks of me is to surrender what I think is supposed to happen. What I think is supposed to happen is dangerous to me and everyone else. When something happens that causes tightness, constriction, controversy, I need to let go. If I don't, I just become part of that contraction.

Anyway, it's not what I want that's important. It's what I need. When I come to an obstacle, a snag, a moment of conflict or obsession, I realize that what I want is not appropriate and I learn to surrender to what I need. I learn to "choose" what is.

When I can't choose what is, I cease to be responsible for my life. I begin to want to project that responsibility outward. Things get tricky.

Always, the solution is to embrace whatever comes to me and be with it until I understand it. That is what it means to be responsible. I am not able to respond until I know where I am.

Grace without surrender is not possible. Surrender says "yes." It says "why not!" It says "trust this; something good will come of it." Surrender is the container into which grace flows.

Grace may not come from us, but it comes to us when we open ourselves to it. Every time we surrender what we want or think is supposed to happen, we make room for Spirit to enter into our hearts and minds.

Laughter and Tears

T HE DAY BEFORE the conference, I forgot my briefcase at my typesetter's office. A friend of my typesetter agreed to bring it to his house if I could meet him there. When I got there, he handed me a brochure and said: "This is what I do." He was a clown! I thought that was interesting, but didn't think more about it until the next day.

The next day, while driving my car, I had a vision of myself leading a meditation at the conference and calling out to the Holy Spirit, who would answer my call as the clown. I called Michael the clown and asked him if he would like to collaborate with me in this adventure during the opening circle. He agreed.

So we arranged to have Michael hidden in the balcony. After the announcements, I began leading the meditation. I explained how the Holy Spirit had told me that He would be here with us during the conference and that, if we called out to Him with enough faith, he would appear right in the midst of us. Of course, people who knew me thought I had gone off the wall. And people who didn't know me were beginning to indulge their worst fears about the conference. "Who is this guy, anyway? Is he for real?"

Well, after really pouring on my best born-again Christian act (not bad for an ex-atheist!), I said I felt the Holy Spirit had come. "Are you here, Holy Spirit?" I asked.

A loud whistle rang out from the balcony. "Here I am. Up here!" Michael the clown then grabbed a ladder, lowered it to the floor below, and began climbing down.

"What did you think I would look like?" he asked the audience, as he made his way to the stage. "I have come to help you see things differently."

Then The Holy Spirit proceeded to help everyone see me differently, calling me up to the stage and placing a large red clown nose and funny glasses on my face. Then he asked others to come up and began dressing them in assorted costumes.

Everyone was in stitches. Michael the clown set the tone for the entire conference. We learned to laugh at ourselves and to have fun. That's why we were there, not to intellectualize and to judge one another, but to enjoy each other's presence, to love, to laugh, and to forgive.

In many ways, the appearance of "The Holy Spirit" was just a foretaste of what was to happen during the conference. Later, I led a workshop entitled "Hearing the Voice of the Holy Spirit." I had been guided to structure the workshop in an experiential way, leaving plenty of room for participation. I started off with a meditation, and some verbal trust building exercises. Before long, people were really opening up to the possibility that Spirit could speak through them without any interference from the ego. There was some profound small group sharing, and then we re-convened our circle of about 75 people.

Turning off the lights, I placed a microphone in the center of the circle and asked people to sit quietly, Quaker-style until they were moved to get up and share something from the heart. There was a long and beautiful silence, followed by the sound of footsteps as someone went to the microphone and expressed her gratitude for this experience. Then there was another wonderful silence, followed by another heart-opening statement. And so it continued, silence and sound, silence and sound, each time going deeper. Some people got up who had never shared before a group. Many speakers were moved to tears, as were their witnesses.

Clearly comfort and safety embraced everyone in the room. It was okay to share anything. It was okay to walk through the fears and step forward to share. It was okay to let the heart speak its simple words of gratitude. It was okay to tremble, to cry, to call out for love.

The voice inside of each one of us that judges ourselves and others was absent from our healing circle. In its place was a deep emotional bond that recognized each person as a brother or a sister. We were abiding in a deep acceptance of one another. We were abiding in the grace that comes from our surrender.

I had no idea how I would close our experience together. We were in such a powerful, such a deep emotional place, words could not do it. Then I remembered some music by Mississippi John Hurt that I had recorded for the opening circle. So I went to the tape player and put on the deep raspy voice of John Hurt, an eighty-year old, self-taught master of the Mississippi delta blues. And as he sang "when I lay my burden down" we all held hands and moved gently to the music, feeling our inner sense of liberation as we had joined together without fear.

Finally, we all sang together "You are my Sunshine," which happened to be the last song on the tape. And as we sang, it suddenly addressed us at many levels of meaning. We were singing to each person in the room, to ourselves, and to God. It was all one movement of Spirit, one all-encompassing address.

Finding a Way to Say Yes

AND SO ON THE WEEKEND WENT, from miracle to miracle. At the end of my workshop I was approached by one of the participants. She handed me a manuscript of her poems and asked me if I would read them. I said that I would, but didn't know if I would have a chance to look at them during the weekend, since I was so busy.

I thought no more about this until I was awakened at 6:00 AM the next morning with the inner direction to "go downstairs and read those poems you got yesterday." I felt like getting up early anyway, so I went down and made a cup of coffee, and opened the manuscript to the first poem. It didn't appeal to me as a poem, but I thought "that would make a great song." I started humming a tune and singing the words of the poem and it seemed to work. So I called my friend Ron who was staying at a local hotel and asked him if he could meet me for an early breakfast and bring his guitar. He gave me a sleepy "okay," and I headed out for the hotel. Once there, we started working on the song, and were soon joined by another Course student at the hotel, who helped us improve the melody. Then, we called up our friends Brit and Christina, who were sched-uled to sing during the Sunday service, and asked them to meet us a few minutes before the service started. We quickly taught them the song, and I asked Tony, the minister, to work us into the service.

Before we performed the song, I gave a brief synopsis of how it had come to be. Of course, every-one loved the song. And Elaine, who had written the poem, was totally blown away.... Another miracle, another gift given and received!

I was beginning to wonder if the wave of joy and joining would ever end. In truth, it did not! And we all found it difficult to say good-bye.

As I look back on what happened, I realize there was a simple formula behind all this miracle making:

- Say YES to yourself.
- Say YES to your brother or sister.
- Say YES to every possibility
  that affirms someone.
- When you want to say no,
  find a way to say YES.
- Even when you have to say no,
  find a way to say YES too.

The Holy Spirit doesn't know how to say "no." That word just does not exist in its vocabulary. "Yes" is love's word. Of course, we are always finding people who are hard to love. And we want to say no to them, but we need to find a way to say yes. We don't start loving until we start saying yes.

That is the magic formula, if there is one.

Everyone is walking with wounds. Everyone expects a "no." Everyone is prepared to say "no" in return. "Yes" begins to heal our wounds. Even when you say no, you can say yes: "I can't respond to the way you are acting now, but I know you are calling out for love. I can't allow you to abuse me. I won't allow you to abuse me. But I see you are hurt. I see you want love but don't know how to ask for it. And I want you to know I think you are worthy of love."

Everyone is walking with wounds and attacking before s/he is attacked first. That is the nature of the illusion we live with.

That is the nature of a world that is fear-based.

"Yes" challenges the world of illusion at its roots. It says: "another world is possible, and I am the way to it." All you have to do is find a way to say yes. And, if you can't say yes yet, then just stop saying no.

Start saying "I don't know" or "I'm not sure" or "the jury's still out and I'm not privy to their conversations." Be neutral.

If you can't love yet, just don't attack.

My friend Paul Kelly tells a beautiful story of how he practiced just that activity. He had taken a job working for some people who were twenty years his junior. They thought they knew everything, even though they had only a fraction of Paul's experience. They used to correct his spelling and overrule his opinion on just about every subject. Paul had just started working with *A Course in Miracles*. He couldn't deal with the whole text, so he just started using this one principle "don't attack, and don't defend." For a year he practiced this principle in his job. And his young associates provided him with many daily opportunities to practice!

In time, Paul's associates started to change their opinion about him. They saw that he did good work. They saw that he didn't get hung up on personality issues. They saw that he had respect for every person. They saw that he had a deep integrity. And so they began to trust him. They began to ask for his advice. Indeed, within a year, their attitude toward Paul had been completely transformed! That's what this simple practice can do.

If you can't love, then just don't hate. If you can't accept, then just don't reject. If you can't say yes yet, then just find a way not to say no.

Sometimes we shoot too high in our spiritual practice. We need to find a practice that we're not intimidated by. Otherwise, we won't use it. It will just be an idea that props us up, but never changes our lives.

The conference suggested over and over again the way of surrender and grace: "just say yes." But it also taught us an important practice: "if you can't say yes, don't say no." This is a practice we can all use. We don't have to be angels to use it. We don't have to be perfect to use it.

In fact, if we insist on being perfect, every yes we say will really be a no. Because to be perfect means to be right all the time. And that means we can't make mistakes.

If we can't make mistakes, then whatever we do won't be enough. Every yes will really be a no. The way of perfection and the way of forgiveness are not the same way.

Only forgiveness brings us to perfection. And forgiveness means making mistakes and learning from them.

Even if we say no, let's find a way to say yes too. Even if we reject, let's find a way to accept. This is our practice. This is our way toward surrender.

The rest is up to the Holy Spirit. If we don't attack or defend, S/he will do the rest. It worked for Paul and it can work for us too. S/he just needs our "little willingness."

PART FOUR

·

Transcending Dualism

"We can't solve our problems from the level of the problem, which is dualistic. We solve our problems only from the standpoint of unity consciousness, which is inclusive of the opposites."

Transcending Dualism

Acceptance as a Unity Teaching

I'LL NEVER FORGET that day when Sean and I had lunch before he left to take the train to Georgia to begin the Appalachian Trail. Vicki had come, but she wanted to give Sean and me time to talk, so she went for a walk. When Sean and I came out of the Coffee Connection, Vicki was sitting on the steps crying.

Years ago, she had wanted to open a restaurant in this building, but she had been turned down by the management. At the time, it seemed like a put-down. But sitting there quietly now Vicki realized that, had she started her restaurant here, it never would have become as successful as it did in her downtown location. So quiet tears of gratitude flowed from her eyes.

Meanwhile, Sean had come to a place where he just needed to be alone and put one foot in front of the other. The king of kindness was leaving for the woods. His decision was awesome. You could feel the anxiety he felt, yet there was no hesitation. It was somehow perfect.

Life was unfolding its rainbow colors. Purpose was unveiled before my eyes. I was blessed to have these brotherly and sisterly examples of courage and acceptance. Each person's life is a gemstone hidden in the mud. When the mud gets washed away, the colors that emerge are mind-boggling.

Yet the mud has its purpose. Without the mud, the gemstone cannot be discovered. In a world of gemstones, nobody knows he is a gemstone. Perhaps that is a metaphor for heaven on earth.

Heaven may be my origin, but the mud of earth helps me remember it. The mud and muck, the mistakes and lessons help me remember. Is it possible to come to a real acceptance of the process, muddy and imperfect as it is or seems to be?

Without acceptance, there can be no forgiveness. And without forgiveness, there can be no learning, no rite of passage, no increase in awareness.

Dualistic teaching methods can help me see that my ego condemns myself and others, but they cannot help me forgive my ego. They cannot help me accept my life as it is. They cannot teach me to bless.

To bless, I must accept my ego and yours. To bless, I cannot make the error real. I cannot judge my judgment.

To bless, I must accept what happens and forgive it. I must be willing to take responsibility for what happens, to work with it and birth it, and then let it go. I must "hold on tightly" and "let go lightly." If I cannot forgive my judgments, my awareness of my ego means nothing. Indeed, my judgment of my judgments shows that I do not truly see them for what they are.

Only a non-dualistic learning framework allows us to embrace the entirety of our lives, including the ego. It says to us "Okay, there is the judge, and the one who judges the judge, and it's endless. It goes on forever, because there is this continual sense that the process is "bad."

When we just see the process and accept it, we remove the idea of "bad." It's just a process that goes on. Seeing it, we distance ourselves somewhat from that process, but we understand that there will be times when we are drawn back into our judgments. So we try to be easy with that, without labeling it, and we try to stay as aware as we can be.

I begin to accept my life as a journey in and out of judgments. I don't make judging "bad" and not judging "good," because that just sets up the duality again. I see the process as completely okay. I see how sometimes judging brings me to awareness and sometimes it prevents me from being aware.

Accepting the process and being with the process helps me stay in the present. And this, of course, is the mystical side of the teaching, because the more I stay in the present, the more I find my judgments just drop away.

Whenever I am feeling anxious or upset, I have moved from being a witness and participant to being a judge. I have moved away from the present, away from the process itself.

We do not find our guidance until we learn to trust the process. Trust assumes that whatever happens will be appropriate. It does not need to direct the future, because the present is sufficient in itself.

As we are increasingly content to stay in the present, we find that we struggle less. We have fewer expectations and fewer disappointments. We just do our best and forgive when that seems to be not enough.

And so we move from the abstract world of ideas to the direct world of experience. We stop talking about "acceptance," and start to practice it. We erase the gap between what we believe and what we experience. We stay with the truth of ourselves. And we become witnesses to the original blessing.

Nothing is
What it Seems

LAST SPRING, when I was still living in Vermont, an interesting omen occurred. During mating season, a robin started flying into the glass of our sliding glass door. Opinion differed as to whether he was trying to mate with his reflection or challenge what he thought was a male intruder. Whatever his motivation was, it was obviously strong, because he refused to go away. Day after day, hour after hour, he threw himself up against the glass, making a loud thud, yet without injuring himself.

My neighbor tried to dissuade him with his bee bee gun, but the bird was too fast and too determined. In the end, we just gave up and learned to live with the noise and the bird poop on the back deck.

Without knowing why, I interpreted this event as a sign that we would be leaving the house we were living in. About a week after the robin had started his kamikaze flights, I left Vermont to spend a few days alone on Cape Cod. When I returned, my wife told me that she had just received a notice from the hospital indicating that she would be laid off along with 26 other employees.

My immediate reaction was that this was a good thing. My wife had been in a job in which she was not truly valued personally or professionally. She had to answer to a boss who had half of her experience and understanding. It was awkward and there was no reason for this to continue.

Soon Marjorie began a nationwide job search. Many colleges and hospitals were interested in her. Of all the possibilities, a job in Hawaii seemed most intriguing. But how would we ever make such a major move? What would we do with all our furniture, our books and records? The thought of trying to move all that stuff was mind boggling. It also became clear that it would be incredibly expensive to do so. And what about the kids, how would they adapt? We had moved several times in the last couple of years, would they be able to handle yet another move, and so far away?

Clearly Hawaii was the most exciting of all the possibilities, but also the one which involved the most challenge. How would we handle the logistics? We decided to test the waters by having a yard sale to see if we could get rid of some of our furniture. That weekend, some twenty or thirty people came through our house and bought about half of everything we owned. We were amazed. For the first time, it became clear that we were Hawaii bound. Shortly thereafter, we found another family to take over our rental lease. And so, within 30 days, our belongings were sold, our cars were packed, and we were off.

While I did not want to remain in Vermont long-term, it was clear that this was not a good time for me to go somewhere else. I had a book and a magazine in production and I was in full swing planning a large conference. So I made the commitment to stay on the east coast for a couple of months to complete these projects. I then joined my family in Hawaii.

The transition was a lot harder that we expected. The cost of living was outrageous. I had to try to run my business from 6,000 miles away. And the kids were feeling insecure from the recent family separation and having trouble adjusting to a new culture. It just did not make sense. Yet, on another level, it must have made sense, because everything that needed to happen to make this move possible happened. The way had simply opened before us and we stepped through the door.

At the time of this writing I still do not know why I am here. I feel that there is a purpose, but I don't know what it is. What I do know is that, in order to survive in this place, we have had to let go of a lot of our ideas about the way life is supposed to be. Indeed, this latest move from New England to the mid-Pacific caps a five year process in which we have given up our house, our furniture and most of our personal possessions. Sometimes we feel guilty about this when we think of the effect it may be having on the kids. Yet we also know that it challenges our deepest emotional resources. It means that we really have to learn to rely on love, because the other sources of security just aren't there.

Clearly, the Holy Spirit is up to something here. Since I don't know what that is yet, all I can do is to endeavor to be as fully present and open as possible. That is a lot easier said than done. Indeed, it is a constant struggle, for I find myself longing for the definition and structure that used to be in my life. I don't feel entirely safe in this "not knowing." How do you put down roots in the middle of the unknown? And what do these roots look like?

The robin who foretold our journey did not know the length or the duration of our flight. Nor did we in embarking. We knew only that the breeze was behind us. And, unbeknownst to us, we had wings that needed to be tested.

My metaphor for strength and flexibility has always been a tree. I am fond of the idea that as the roots go deeper, the tree can reach further into the sky. It is a balanced, earthy image of spirituality. But this is changing now. Roots are giving way, not just to branches, but to wings. The tree is getting ready for the next phase of its journey. Its seedlings catch the wind and sail out over the meadow, knowing not where they will fall. They go where the wind takes them. They go where they are needed. That is the way my life seems to me now.

The roots the seedling sets are fragile. They can be easily disturbed. The fury of life — sudden vortices of fire and air — takes its toll on the young saplings. Yet some survive and stronger roots anchor them to the nurturing embrace of earth and water. Now the seed's journey is done. Now the tree asserts itself. Its main branches grow large, supporting hundreds of smaller branches, supporting a brocade of leaves.

We are drawn to the tree. It gives us a cool spot to sit quietly away from the afternoon sun. Children find its welcoming limbs, while their parents watch anxiously. Under the canopy of the tree poems are born, and paintings fixed in the mind. Old people sit in the shade of the tree, watching the pageantry of a life that gently shifts away from them. There is a deep nurturing presence here, a holding of all things in patient surrender. This tree, which began as a seedling, broken by fire and hurled on the wind, has come to its own fulfillment. It blesses all who sit beneath it and play in its branches. This tree, that never once knew the outcome, that rode the fiery wind through oblivion to find the gentle kiss of water and earth, this tree speaks to us a simple truth:

"There is always a blessing hidden
in your life waiting for you to find it."

So in this moment we do not know what will come. The past fades, losing its grip upon the mind, and the future stirs mysteriously, moving like a mercurial wind through the open doors of the heart. We have come to this place suddenly, not knowing why, and we remain, not able to anticipate even a single moment of it.

Roots have become wings. And wings have found anchor in the mind's growing silence. Something stirs, but we don't know what it is. A robin hits the glass repeatedly, starting a tidal wave thousands of miles away. The dream dips and slides, its inhabitants waking at odd hours of the night. It is all one long shadowy blessing, one thought in the mind giving way to that which is beyond thought.

We Choose
the Lesson

THE CONSTRUCTIVE NATURE of change in our lives cannot be appreciated so long as we see the form in which that change comes as an attack on us. Inevitably, the change process strips away some aspect of our lives which has become superfluous or burdensome. And allowing the process to work in our lives without judgment of ourselves or others is essential. Otherwise, we will take an impersonal process and add our own personal meaning to it. That will merely cloud our lesson, which is a simple one: it's time to let our burdens go.

We must remember that everything that happens to us, yes EVERYTHING, is part of the plan for our awakening. It is easy to forget this. It is easy to feel that we are victims of what happens, because that demands nothing from us.

What we do not know is that it is our own desire for freedom and intimacy which asks for the wake up call. It does not come without our permission. From deep within the illusion, we call for truth. From deep within our pain, we call for peace. From deep within our co-dependency and self-denial, we call for the freedom to be who we are.

We all forget that we are the architects of the buildings we inhabit. That's okay. The dreamer gets lost in his own dream for a while. Then he gets a wake up call. At first, he is angry. The dream may be lousy, but he's used to it. He's not ready to shift gears, yet that is what he is asked to do. That is what he asked himself to do when he lay down to sleep.

When we resist what life offers us, we know we have forgotten that we asked for it. We have replaced what we need with what we want and inwardly we know this. Inwardly, we know a shift must occur. We must address our needs, not our wants. We must stop needing what we want, and learn to want what we need. That is the direction of our freedom. That is the direction of our growth.

It is hard to realize that we put ourselves in prison. We are so good at building four walls and a roof, we forget all about the earth and the sky. We block off our own energy, our very life line. Fortunately, we have the key to the door of our prison cell. We're just afraid to use it. It is scary out there in the world. There's all that energy and it's so unpredictable!

We need to realize that it's okay to be afraid. A woman who recognizes her fear will not need to rebuild her prison. Nobody ever got into trouble by acknowledging her fear.

It's not fear that is problematic. It's what we do with our fear! Denial, projection, and attack institutionalize fear. That is why so much of our experience is fear-based. When we deny our fears, everything we do is subconsciously influenced by them.

A healthy person acknowledges his fears. A healthy couple looks at its fears. A healthy society admits its fears.

We get stuck holding onto our fears precisely because we try to make them go away. That is an important lesson.

Truth often comes by way of paradox or irony. That is because our understanding is dualistic. We want black and white, either/or choices. Our very perception of the world prevents our understanding of it. So along comes an event that says "both are equal" or "gray wins" and it throws us completely off. But that's exactly what we need. We can't solve our problems from the level of the problem, which is dualistic. We solve our problems only from the standpoint of unity consciousness, which is inclusive of the opposites.

The challenge for us is a simple one, even though it isn't so simple to meet. It asks us to stay with what's happening, because we created it. We made the lesson so that we could learn it. And we did a good job. We made it with so much integrity that we made sure we would not be able to get off cheap. We made it so we would have to go down deep to learn it. And that, of course, is why it seems so hard. It has been set up perfectly.

Each one of us needs to come to appreciate our collusion in this great drama! We ask for our lessons and we get them. Whenever something happens that unsettles our lives, we need to remember that we are the architect of the reality that faces us. True, we may have hired a builder to build our house, but the builder just builds from a set of plans. The real question is: who designed the plans?

We are both the dreamer and the one who comes to wake the dreamer up. May we remember this when the wake up call comes.

In and Out of Boxes

W E'RE ALWAYS DEFINING and predicting, looking toward the future or back to the past. There are very few moments when we stop resisting what's happening in our lives. Yet those are the moments when we begin to see with real insight.

When I let go of my expectations of the future, I stop carrying my past forward. I diffuse the intensity of the karmic flow in my life. I develop an attitude of reverence, of receptiveness, of waiting to see. I realize that I really don't know what anything is for.

I have a sense of what is happening. But I don't really know the width and breadth of it. In fact, often I am totally fooled. Forms that I believe to be substantial float away as my hands reach out to touch them. Feelings I thought were vanquished rise from their unsavory resting place and stand awkwardly in my path.

Everything I have buried is eventually unearthed. And everything I have sought outside me comes to nought. But this is not a punishment.

This is just a reckoning.

I stand in front of a mirror. Nothing more or less. The eyes I see look back at me. The people I condemn or bless recognize me.

If there's anything I'm afraid to look at, my life

will show it to me. But that's not to wound me. That's just to show me the full play of consciousness. That's to show me how I limit my reality, and how I expand beyond those limits.

You know, my greatest fear is to look at myself. I'm convinced that when I do that, I'm going to see dreadful things. I don't want to look at me. I'd rather look at you.

And that's what I try to do. That's the illusion. I try to look at you. I try to relate to myself, positively and negatively, through you. But my journey has nothing at all to do with you until I have learned to look at myself.

As long as the warp and woof of my life is played out around your needs or my needs in relation to you, I'm refusing to look in the mirror. Your only purpose in my life is to be a mirror for me, whether you understand that or not.

Everything begins with me. Everything begins in my own consciousness. Everything begins with the choices I make moment to moment. All that seems to involve you, but it does so only tangentially. You are not a cause or a result of the choices I make. You are not responsible for what I choose. You are not a victim of what I choose. All that belongs to illusion. All that is a refusal to look in the mirror.

I cannot begin to see who you are until I face myself. I must face what I don't like about myself and forgive it. I must face what I like too much about myself and forgive it. I must face all the assumptions, all the beliefs that live in my mind. That's what my journey is.

As I face these beliefs, I see how each one limits my reality. It doesn't matter what those beliefs are. Any belief limits my reality, because any belief is a prejudice. Any belief imposes an artificial structure on the free flow of experience.

Every belief is just a box I jump into. When I'm in the box, I see only what's inside the box. "Meaning" exists only inside the box. Outside the box, there is no meaning, or if there is a meaning I don't know what it is. Inside the box, I think I know. Outside the box, I know I don't know.

My journey here is a journey in and out of boxes. The more boxes I leave behind, the more free I become, the more open I become, the more accepting I become. Every time I leave a box behind, I leave biases and attachments behind.

All of us find our boxes comforting. They are predictable. But, when you think of it, the only thing that is predictable is pain. Joy is not predictable! Have you ever tried to predict joy? You can't do it. Joy just happens. It is an experience. You can't anticipate it. You can't repeat it. You can't control joy in any way.

Only pain is predictable, yet strangely we are attached to our pain. That is how deep our guilt runs. We choose our pain over and over again, because we think that if we don't we will experience a greater pain. We choose a chronic pain to escape what we fear will be a sudden, excruciating pain. We choose slow death, slow crucifixion, over sudden death. Because sudden death is a complete unknown.

We choose what we know. We choose the past. We keep the illusion going.

The only thing we have to do to leave the illusion behind is to stop referencing the past. It is that simple.

When we allow everything that ever happened to us to be completely embraced and accepted, it ceases to have consequence. It only has consequence (karma) as long as we refuse to accept it.

Accepting everything of duality (our entire experience here) helps us move to the unity experience. Without acceptance, unity cannot be experienced.

The mind that judges and condemns cannot apprehend unity. Unity is experienced only as we accept our judgments and forgive them. This brings us to the gateway of transcendence.

That is all we can do. That is as far as we can go. Like Moses, we look out over the promised land. We cannot travel there.

All we can do is move out of the box.

All we can do is look in the mirror.

All we can do is see our limitations and step beyond them.

The Empty Mirror

EVERY RELEASE is an unburdening of what's in the mind. What's in the mind does not belong to the mind. The mind is a channel. It is empty. Content flows in and out. But mind is not the content.

Attachment to content fills the emptiness. It fills the silence. It complicates and confuses. It interrupts and contradicts. For every thing that we want, there's some thing we don't want. Attachment to content is an attempt to control what cannot be controlled.

We want to control the flow of consciousness, but it cannot be done. We can discipline the mind, exercise it like a muscle, even get it to perform magic tricks, but we can never really control the content of consciousness. At best, we focus on certain things and repress others. But what is repressed does not go away.

It is impossible to control the content of consciousness. It comes and it goes. You cannot know why it comes or why it goes. You cannot determine when it comes or when it goes. The idea that you can influence what comes up is magical thinking. Healing does not come from magical thinking. It comes from surrender.

When I surrender to what comes up, I keep the mind flexible. Whatever happens is okay as it is. I don't have to like it. I don't have to dislike it. I just need to accept it. Or if I can't accept it, I just need to accept the fact that I don't accept it.

Surrender means I stop taking issue with life. I stop needing to alter it. I am content to experience what happens. That is enough.

As we work with surrendering, we encounter our resistance. There is a part of us that holds on, or denies, or runs away. We feel injured, abandoned, anxious or disappointed by what happens. We feel victimized. We feel angry.

Whether we like it or not, our resistance comes up. Every time we surrender ego, more ego comes up. That is the nature of the process. It doesn't mean that we're doing the process incorrectly. It just means we're going deeper with it.

Resistance makes us self-conscious. We're not content any more just being a channel. We need to call ourselves a channel, or compare our experience with that of others. And as soon as we do this, we stop channeling.

In a state of surrender, there is no self-consciousness. There is no need to stand back and judge. There is no need to anticipate the direction of the energy. There is just openness. There is just willingness.

Mind can be thought of as a perfect mirror, capable of reflecting whatever comes before it. It is the mirror, not the reflection. The objects, situations, emotions and events that are reflected by the mind do not describe what the mind is.

Mind is universal, that is to say it is by nature open and inclusive. Yet we know that the world appears differently to each observer. Each person determines what he sees and experiences according to what he believes.

Beliefs indicate conditions. But mind is unconditional. No system of beliefs can describe the nature of mind itself, which is empty and without form. Only the reflections of mind appear to have form.

The nature of mind is perfect peace, perfect acceptance. Because it is capable of reflecting all things, it cannot but accept the full spectrum and variety of what it reflects. Mind itself is incapable of judgment.

Judgment is a constriction of mind, or a belief. It doesn't matter what the belief is about. It still constricts mind. It still narrows perfect peace, perfect acceptance. It still mistakes the form for the content.

The spiritual practice "neti, neti (not this, not that)" helps to build an awareness of the mirror itself by withdrawing the attention from the reflections. The question "what is the nature of consciousness when it is at rest?" anticipates the nature of mind itself.

I have a poem that goes:

> "When the cycle of doing
> comes to an end,
> things fall back on themselves.
> With nothing to prop them up,
> only their essence remains."

The essence of mind is silence. It is the medium in which sound travels. Mind is the container.

When mind identifies with its content, it becomes

caught in the cycle of doing, the river of causality. It becomes subject to the contradictory ideas with which it identifies. This is the world we live in.

Every consciousness creates the reality in which it finds itself, and that reality is by nature limited. It is by nature hurtful. It is by nature dualistic and self-conscious. There is nothing that can be done about this. You can't change the illusion on the level of the illusion.

Yet at the same time that we are caught in this vast interconnecting net of illusion, mind is free of all of it. Indeed, without mind, none of it would exist.

Our part in this drama is simply (it is not so simple, really) to be aware of our beliefs and their effects. The more awareness we bring to our own attachments, the more they begin to fall away, and the more the container opens.

The role of Spirit is simply (it is simple, really) to move toward any container that is open to it. This happens automatically. We don't even have to ask for it.

The existence of the unconditional energy of Spirit must be verified experientially by each person. It is not something that can be taught intellectually. At best, any description of Spirit is a pointer toward the experience.

The practice of surrender, however, brings concrete results. One need only be willing to try it to reap the rewards. In meditation, let the mind detach from the content that moves through it. In working or driving or playing or dreaming or sleeping, let the mind say "neti, neti, (not this, not that)." Let the mind rest upon itself. Let the mirror be empty.

As you practice, relax. Let events come and go. Let thoughts and feelings come and go. The more you relax, the more empty you become, and the more purpose can flow through you. Gradually, you'll find that whatever needs to be done can be done through you, because you are not personally attached to it.

So every moment becomes an opportunity to surrender, to connect with a purpose that transcends our conceptual limits. Every moment becomes an opportunity to toss out old definitions, to drop expectations, to be present, and to be of help.

PART FIVE

Living and Dying

"Born from what I
think is my hardest
time is a jewel
of awareness.
Everything perceived
apart is seen together,
the whole drama
of right and wrong,
self and other,
desire and fear."

———————•———————

Living and Dying

Reverie

I AM TERRIFIED BY DEATH, and yet I know that death is part of life. Death is a release of the past. In death, I go beyond everything I know.

Death is fearful to me, because I still feel a little guilt. This tiny bit of guilt convinces me that death means extinction. In death, I will exist no more.

I am afraid of my own extinction. I am afraid of the hand that lifts the breath from my lungs and leaves behind a heap of flesh and bones, a carcass for scavengers and worms.

The future of the body is bleak. The future of the mind, as I know it, is also bleak. None of this will remain when I have gone. This world will disappear. These ideas and feelings that have created my perception of the world will disappear.

I will be an empty slate, no longer conscious of myself as a separate entity. The ability to know through separation will no longer exist. If there is knowledge, it will be a kind of knowledge I have not experienced.

It does not matter how much I talk myself into death as a benign experience for me. It does not matter how hard I work to make death a metaphor, rather than a visceral experience. All this is just chatter to stave off the fear. All this is just denial.

I must face my death now, in this moment. I must meet the retreat of blood and breath with an advance of Spirit. What I am must come forth. What I am must be born, now.

Death is a birth into another life I know nothing of. It is a movement beyond projection, beyond separation. It is a letting go of conditions, a movement of the river into the awesome clutch of the sea.

Death has me now by a hero's hand. And I plummet down the slope into the cold waters, lit only by moonlight. I swim with my fears to some apparent shore, where I stand up out of the water, exhausted. I walk the beach looking for signs of life. Nothing stirs. The silence is total.

I look down for my body, but I cannot find it. I walk without walking, drifting as by ideas from one place to another. When I begin to feel I am lost, an unseen hand reaches out to steady me. I grasp it firmly, as if holding it could help me confirm my own existence.

Each step requires faith. Each step takes me to the doorstep of another dream. Yet I remain in a corridor between two worlds. Ominous shapes pass by, all projections of my own fears. Even as I feel the contraction in my entrails, I know that these phantoms cannot hurt me. I know God cannot attack me.

Now a door appears suddenly in the black wall and the unseen hand opens it. Still afraid, I walk through it. This much I can do. This much I have done before. Never have I been punished for walking through my fear.

Once on the other side, I cannot describe where I am. Words are inadequate. Truth is fully present, but not detachable from its context. Pain lives side by side with unexpected joy.

To gain this place you must be able to join, yet willing to enter by yourself. Here, alone means "all one." Each being must come to this in her own way, in her own time. Each one must find the place where the boundaries fall away. Each must cross over the river of death and sin.

And on the other side, those whom we took for dead are raised up from their jagged sleep. White lilies bloom along the roadside of the vineyard, where the grapes are harvested and pummeled under feet. All this seems to be a dream, but something says not. Something says "stay alert."

A landscape without bodies is a landscape of love incarnate. Dances are danced in the open field. Poems are read under the stars at the breakwater's edge.

Forms are broken and reassembled again by the consciousness that made them, a patchwork quilt of lessons learned and waiting to be learned. Where space ends, the river of time begins all over again, snaking down from the mountain into the valley below.

In the struggle of form, peace is found and permeates all things. This blessing runs like an underground stream at the base of the skull. Unexpected, it opens the hill of the forehead and trickles down the nose and the lips, a nectar made in the bowels of the earth.

Born from what I think is my hardest time is a jewel of awareness. Taken from the muddy mandrake root, the holy breath and final blessing. Everything perceived apart is seen together, the whole drama of right and wrong, self and other, desire and fear.

The train of time rushes down the hillside and comes to rest halfway up the next hill. When the engine stops, everything finds its level. Passengers disembark on unfamiliar ground.

I have seen something like this in a movie, *Elvira Madigan* I think: lovers moving in slow motion through a field of wildflowers, their steps flowing from the lilting sounds of the Andante from Mozart's piano concerto number Number 21 in C Major. The whole rush of time, the whole confusion of space brings us to this ecstatic moment where life and death touch, indelibly.

Shifting Sands

THE WIND BLOWS and the sands shift. It is still the same amount of sand, but arranged in a different position. The wind blows and the sands shift. That is how it is with consciousness.

Recently, my friend Michael made a commitment to working with his music. Then fear set in. He felt the compulsion to find a job. He felt the compulsion to make money, buy a house, and so on. He was ready to let his commitment to his music go.

The wind blows and the sands shift. A single visit from his father, a few words from his wife, and the deep-set guilt made a run for the surface. He saw it coming, but didn't know what it was. Suddenly, he was saying things like "I'll never be able to support myself doing my music. I've been irresponsible all my life. I can't take time off now. I'm just deluding myself. I've got to grow up, take responsibility." What began as a willingness to trust a deeply buried gift became in a flash permission to feel an old fear.

That was the lesson. The fear must be felt. It must be acknowledged. The guilt must be seen for what it is, a denial of self, a distrust of the gift.

It is no different for Michael than it is for any one of us. We each carry our "sweet sword of revenge." Whenever we trust enough to step out of our own conceptual boxes, we find that we are attacked by this mysterious sword. Generally, we just feel the contraction of our fear and quickly step back inside our box. But, if we don't, if we look carefully, we will see that we hold the sword ourselves.

Others may judge us, but we are the ones who hold the judgments or let them fall away. If we are honest, we will admit that there is not a single person among us who hasn't placed obstacles in the way of his or her emancipation. Other people and outside forces seem to have a role in this, and we like to blame them to justify our move back into the box, but deep down we know that we were the ones who gave permission. We were the ones who stepped back in the face of our own guilt.

If I believe there is something wrong with me, if I see myself as a failure, as inadequate in any way, I will build bars around my life. I will decide what I can't do and be limited by that belief. To think that I don't do this is naive. I do this all the time.

You do this all the time.

That's okay. It's not important to stop doing this. That just becomes a different game we can lose. We can keep on doing what we have to do at the time, but we must begin to see what that is. We must begin to take responsibility for the limits we place on our lives. Only when we begin to own our role in making the box do we begin to see that we can empower ourselves to step out of it. After all, anyone who can make a box can unmake it.

Box-making and box un-making are the warp and woof of our illusory journey here. In truth, none of these boxes exist, except in our own minds. And it is in our own minds that they must be erased.

For all intents and purposes the limits we create are real to us until we step beyond them. Then they cease to be real. We would like to believe that there is a "process" of stepping out, a "process of denying the illusion," but there is no such thing. There is either the step back, or the step forward. There is either the capitulation to guilt, or the willingness to walk through the fear that stands behind the guilt.

When I think that there is something wrong with me — and it really doesn't matter "what" I think is wrong with me — I am really saying that I am afraid of my power. Have I misused that power before in my life? Perhaps. We all do misuse our power until we realize that our power is vertical not horizontal. As long as we think we are powerful in relationship to anyone else, we misunderstand our power.

So I may believe that I will hurt someone else if I give myself permission to do what I want to do. In other words, if I honor myself, I will hurt others. So I don't trust myself for fear of making a bad mistake. I'm afraid that I'll screw up, so I deny myself the lesson I have come to learn.

I have come to learn to love myself and others, but I can't learn how to do this because I'm unwilling to make mistakes. And I can't learn as long as I'm unwilling to make mistakes.

This is a very clear Catch 22. This is the kind of box we make for ourselves emotionally. We may not be, indeed often are not, consciously aware of the box. We suffer from the box. We function and see the world from the box. But we don't know the box is there.

We don't know that the central issue in our lives is that we are afraid of our own power. And our fear of our own power is the same fear as the fear of God.

We are afraid of God because we are afraid of ourselves. If we could do anything we wanted to do, we might hurt people. After all, that's what Hitler did. That's what Saddam Hussein did. Our secret fear is that we would do the same thing if given license. And indeed, there's evidence to support that belief. Look at what happened at that Yale experiment. When people were given permission to inflict pain on other human beings, they did so. When violence is condoned by society, people do not hesitate to express it.

So our distrust of ourselves runs very deep. And with good reason, my friend Judy would say!

But we must understand how this collective guilt affects our individual lives. As long as we think power is external and must play itself out in our relationships, we will be afraid of ourselves, afraid of others, and afraid of God. It is all one fear: fear of the Self.

But Self is not external. Personality is external. It is not who I am, but who I think I am which has the capacity for sin.

In the world, misunderstandings prevail. I don't trust myself because the person I think I am is fearful and guilty. I don't trust you for the same reason. Needless to say, if I am so skeptical about you and I, I am no less skeptical about God.

But this God is a god of my own creation. And this person I think I am or I think you are is a person of my own creation.

The world I see has absolutely no objectivity about it. It is entirely a product of my imagination. And that is true of every person I perceive including myself.

I really don't know who I am or who you are! That's the truth. And the only way I come to know anything is through trust, through "my willingness" to allow my thoughts and feelings to express and be shared.

As long as I would keep my internal world separate from yours, as long as I insist on that kind of privacy, I will see a subjective world of my own making. Only when I trust myself to disclose and to listen to your disclosure without judgment do I begin to experience the real world, the world of communication and communion.

In the real world, I am innocent and so are you. In the real world both of us are trustworthy. In the real world, my talent is not a threat to yours. There is no competition, no greed, no struggle for ego validation.

The real world can be experienced. With acceptance and trust, one sees the guilt come up without buying into it. One feels the contraction of fear, without stepping backward.

I see that I have a belief that I am bad, but I challenge that belief. I see that I am afraid of my power because I have abused it. I see that I must learn what power really is, and I am ready to learn. I am ready to move from the subjective world of self-doubt and mistrust to the objective world of innocence and truth.

The former world I made. The latter world was given me to live in. But living there was not so easy a task as I thought.

So Michael and I sit by the pond, with night coming on. As the sun sinks down behind the Dummerston hills, the shadows of the trees deepen on the water. Tonight he has heard a different voice, the voice of his innocence. And he knows it is a different voice.

Still the choice is his. He will decide which voice he must listen to. From the perspective of the world, my counsel of "trust" is insane. It is irresponsible. From the perspective of love and acceptance, the counsel of guilt is insane. It is simply the result of a fear that must sooner or later be experienced, a contraction that must be ridden out so that the next step can be taken.

Michael's struggle is not with the world, but with two voices inside his own mind. Jesus heard those voices when he was in the desert. Everyone is tested in this way.

To move forward authentically, one must leave everything that is inauthentic behind. One must say "no" to self-limitation and guilt, before one can say "yes" to the flowering of Self. One must reject the past which is filled with images of manipulation and mistrust, to move psychologically to a place beyond fear.

The world offers a guarantee of temporary security: a job, a house, a family, a routine, all for the simple price of self denial. The material rewards of capitulation are great, for the world supports those who conform to its norms.

But the spiritual life, the quest for authentic experience, is not about conformity to norms. It is about breaking the habit patterns that limit experience. It is about expansion beyond the boundaries of what is known. It leaves the past behind. It abandons the future.

It asks each of us but one question: "Are you loving yourself right now." And upon this question, all the others rest.

Catching Up
With Time

THE ONLY THING that is predictable about time is that you can never catch up to it. The future is always ahead of you and the past is always behind you. No matter how hard you try, you cannot bring either one into the present.

At best, you can bring yourself into the present. In those rare moments when you or I do that, past and present fall away in opposite directions, like twin shells of an egg, leaving only the yolk. Being in the present is being in a timeless state, a state free of guilt about the past, or expectation about the future.

I remember when I was going through a crisis in my real estate business. I owned property, but the property would not sell. So my assets meant very little. I had no cash to work with, so I couldn't extricate myself from debt. In a paper world, I had gone from a position of apparent strength to a position of apparent weakness. Whenever I thought about my situation, I felt depressed, drained of energy.

When I woke up in the morning and saw the sun rise out over the marsh, I was filled with energy and optimism. But a single phone call from a bill collector would bring me back into a downward spiral. Finally, I realized that I could do absolutely nothing about my external situation, but I could do something about my state of mind. I began a very simple practice. I said to myself "my present happiness is my only responsibility." Whenever a situation came up which disturbed my peace — feeling guilt about the past or anxiety about the future — I remembered this sentence. And I continued to use it as a mantra whenever I needed it. Indeed, it was a lifesaver for me.

Others wondered how I could be so calm when my life seemed to be falling apart in front of me. The answer was clear. I knew that I couldn't run my life any more. All I could handle was staying in the moment. As soon as I veered away from the moment, I lost my peace. And losing my peace was not just a mild irritation; it was a major psychological nose dive. So my mantra really was my lifeline.

To some extent, my situation has remained the same during the last few years. Many times the external factors looked bleak. In one year, for example, I had to move my family with all our belongings three times. And then my wife lost her job, and we were looking at another move. In the face of all this turbulence, my only guide has been an inner steadiness, an awareness that I can be centered and happy in the moment, regardless of the external factors of my life.

Right now, I can be happy. And if I am happy, it does not matter what the world is doing or not doing. My happiness is a function of my being in the present without anxiety or guilt. Heaven is right now, right here. It is not yesterday (most of us know that!) and it is not tomorrow (we're just beginning to realize that too!)!

I cannot be in the present and not be happy. Happiness is synonymous with the simple act of being present without judgment. As soon as judgment enters, I am jettisoned into the past.

In the past, I judge myself. I judge you. In the past I see nothing but lack. That is true because the past can never catch up to the present. The conditions of the past, good or bad, cannot truly be carried forward to the present, except in our own minds.

Nostalgia about the past is an attempt to make the past more palatable then it was when we experienced it. This is one way to avoid the present. Guilt about the past is an attempt to make the past seem worse than it was when we experienced it. This is another way to avoid the present.

Meanwhile, the truth is that the past is past. Whatever it was it is. I cannot change what happened. I can only change how I feel about it. The only way I can work with the past is in the present. That is the essence of the forgiveness process.

Only in the present can I forgive. I cannot forgive the past in the past. I cannot forgive with the consciousness of the one who committed the mistake. I can only forgive with the consciousness of the one who sees the mistake and is willing to learn from it. I can only forgive when I know that forgiveness is necessary. And only in this moment is such an awareness possible.

Learning to be in the moment is the ultimate

lesson that we all face. For only in the moment are we whole and free. Only now are we innocent.

In the past, we are guilty. In the future, we are condemned to die. Only now can we live, as we are, without apology.

We like to believe that our lives are linear, moving quietly, if not somewhat deliberately, on a straight path from birth to death. But this is just a metaphor we accept. It is not the only metaphor.

The horizontal, linear journey takes us toward some goal we cherish. It is concerned with form, with achievement, with structure. The vertical path keeps us in orbit around an inner center. It is cyclical and repetitive. As we move outward, the gravity of the center pulls us in. The same lesson comes back again and again.

Sometimes it comes back in a familiar form. Sometimes it comes back in a form we don't recognize. In the former case, the form helps us learn the lesson. In the latter case, it teaches us that the lesson is much deeper than the form that carries it. Just because the form is different does not mean that the lesson has changed.

What appears on the surface of our lives may not mean what it seems to mean. That is why, to remain in the present, interpretation must be suspended. Direct knowledge comes not from interpretation, but from acceptance. When the form is accepted simply as it is, without interpretation, its content will be revealed.

Because the mind is not cluttered with judgments, it is capable of direct intuitive apprehension of the form and its content. The form ceases to be dense. It becomes transparent. This is the meaning of the word "revelation."

Revelation happens only in the present. It is a concrete experience of joy, abundance, innocence and perfection. Nothing is lacking, because there is no past to compare it to, either positively or negatively. And because there is no past, and no lack, there is no need for a future.

Right in the midst of conditioned life is the unconditional. Right in the midst of all the ups and downs is a bliss that radiates simultaneously in all directions. We do not have to die to find this place, for it is right here where we stand. But our interpretations of where we stand must die, for they prevent us from being fully present.

"My only responsibility is my present happiness." About the past, I do not know. About the future, I do not know. Nor can I be responsible for what I do not know. I can be responsible only for finding my peace in this moment.

Divinity and Humanity

HOW AM I TO TALK about my Divinity when I cannot even accept my humanness? Until I can accept the fact that I make decisions that create problems for myself and those I care about, I cannot talk about spirituality.

In my spirituality, I aspire to be free of discontent. I yearn to be peaceful and fulfilled. But I do not always live up to my expectations of myself. I feel hurt. I feel pain. I feel inadequate. I feel betrayed. That is part of my journey here. It is part of the human experience.

To deny this "negative" aspect of my experience is to sanitize my life, to pretend to be something I am not. This denial of my darkness may temporarily make me feel better about my life, but my new found ego-brace is bound to be short-lived. As long as I am able to support this artificial "positive" image of myself, as long as I can hoodwink you into seeing and responding only to this part of me, I feel okay. But as soon as my image of self is undermined by strong feelings and aberrant behavior, I fall very quickly from favor with myself and with you.

Whatever I deny I inevitably attract into my life. If I deny my anger, I attract anger toward me, or I attract a disease that attacks me seemingly without mercy. The anger I repress erupts from within my body, like a stream that breaks the dam that holds it back. The anger I project returns like a boomerang to confront me.

In my madness, my sanitized self would attend to your wounds. I would heal you so I don't have to look at my own festering wounds. My dishonesty is not intentional. It is an unconscious tool of my denial. I'd rather place the spotlight on you than upon myself.

My spirituality is a defense against my humanness. I cannot accept the full range of my experience or yours. I have to edit my life for your approval. I have to pretend to be what I am not. Hypocrisy is the price I pay for denial of my humanness.

Yet even an "unhealed healer" such as I can be healed. But the basis of my healing must be what undoes my denial. I must move from repression/projection to self-disclosure. I must admit my mistakes to myself and to you. I must confess my error, my sin. Confessing my error removes it from me.

I hold onto my error only by denying it. Confession is the opposite of denial. It is the medicine I need to overcome my secrecy and my guilt.

In confessing, I expose my guilt. Exposing it helps me to see it and own it. I look at my error and my guilt together and separately. I see that my error can be addressed easily enough. There is a strategy for making amends. But the motivation to make amends will not come until I have forgiven myself. Until I am able to forgive myself, my guilt will hold the error hostage. Acceptance of my darkness is necessary to bring my mistakes into the light of correction. I need not be perfect in my behavior, but I must be willing to see what I have done. To see is not to condemn, but to acknowledge and correct.

If in seeing I condemn, I meet my guilt again. And then I know there is more forgiveness work to do.

I am not bad because I am guilty, although I believe that I am. I must see my guilt and work it through. No one else can do this for me. In the end, I release myself. I must understand this.

Some people promise me the acceptance I cannot give to myself. They are but tempters. Their promises are empty. If I believe them, I will find that emptiness when I reach out.

No one else can condemn me for my mistake, nor can anyone else release me from my guilt. I must wrestle with all the shadowy figures in my mind until I see them for what they are.

The devil is not some demon, but an angel in disguise. Banished to the lower depths, he is the guardian of that world, yet he is not of it. All who accept the authority of sin are content to live by the rules of Hell. But those who have the courage to make the journey through their guilt can leave this world behind for the world of innocence and love.

Heaven is the place of release, even as Hell is the place of bondage. But our images of Heaven and Hell do not help us awaken to the fact that each world is of our own choosing.

Each of us believes he is a devil incarnate. And we spend all our time dressing up in garments that would disguise our fall from grace. We would do better to admit our beliefs. We would do better to see the darkness that gathers to our wings. For then we might remember what those wings are for.

Every man and woman has a devil inside, an angelic being condemned to live among the shadows. To acknowledge this winged being is our most courageous act. For s/he is the one most maligned, attacked and imprisoned by our fear.

We cannot discover our angelic origin if we are afraid to confront the shadowy terrain within our own minds. Each of us must descend to the place where our fears incarnate and there undo them for all time. This is not sanitized work. We have to take off our three piece suits and high heel shoes. Work gloves, old jeans, and rubber boots are the dress code of choice.

Our spirituality is not something we gain in the skies. It is something we win in the trenches of daily life. That may not be consoling, but it is the truth. Better to realize it now than later.

If I would speak of my divinity, let me first accept myself as a human being. Let me see my errors and correct them. Let me see my guilt and forgive it.

Then my words will have meaning. Then my words and my deeds will not conflict.

Then I can meet you as an equal, without needing to raise myself up or put you down, without demanding something from you that you cannot give or feeling betrayed when you cannot keep your promises. An authentic person is not someone spectacular. She is not larger than life, but equal to it.

An authentic person is one who has confronted

hypocrisy in herself. S/he does not need to pretend to be terribly wonderful or overly weak. S/he is just a brother or sister, easy to talk to, willing to embrace the dichotomies of her life, taking pain together with joy, woundedness with wings.

Somewhere it is said that a human being is half devil, half angel. As such, his descent to hell is the same distance as his ascent to heaven. Each part of the journey is essential. If it were not, he would not seek a world of duality to learn in.

Only when both sides of the coin have been experienced is its value fully recognized. If there ever was an argument for cooperation, it must be this one!

The Search for Our Divine Parents

"*Jesus came as the harbinger of a new relationship with the Father. He embodied that relationship and sought to extend it through his relationship with us.*"

———•———

———•———

The Search for Our Divine Parents

Finding the Father

O UR SEARCH for the Divine Father becomes all the more urgent for both men and women in light of our lack of fathering growing up. The father's embrace approves and supports. His discipline helps us develop a sense of relevance and practicality. He helps us take our ourselves seriously, supporting us as we find a way to express our creative purpose in the world.

Without the father, there would be no aspiration, no mountains to climb, no boundaries to safely test, no limitations to overcome. Without the father, we would stay stuck in the womb of co-dependent relationships. We would forsake exploration and adventure, remaining in a familiar place, even as the food supply gets low. Without the father, we would not understand how to end one phase of our life and take up another.

The Jewish Old Testament God evoked one side of the father. He was a God who rewarded those who listened to Him and punished those who did not. He was a jealous god, a god that inspired awe, not love. Some men are like Yahveh. They teach aspiration, discipline, and boundaries. But they do not teach love and so they do not find it.

Jesus brought us a new image of God the Father. To Jesus, Father was friend, nurturer, and witness. The idea of a father who could nurture was foreign to us and still is after two thousand years. Jesus came as the harbinger of a new relationship with the Father. He embodied that relationship and sought to extend it through his relationship with us.

The God of Jesus offered us a personal relationship. We could talk directly to God, as Moses or Abraham had done. There was no need for priests or intermediaries. Father was approachable. We simply needed to hold Him in our hearts and He would speak to us.

Needless to say, it did not take long for the Christians to take the God of Jesus and re-form him back into the Old Testament God.

For only a detached, angry, unapproachable God supports the organizational hierarchy of church or synagogue. Only a God who inspires fear keeps people's behavior in line and insures a steady flow of cash into the coffers. And so Jesus' God of forgiveness has become once again a god of sin, guilt and retribution. The God of unconditional love has become a god of specialness. Nothing has changed.

Men react to an angry father. Some become like the father: jealous, angry, overbearing, good at making judgments, taking control, managing others, but lousy at finding love. Others withdraw from the energy of the father. They are hesitant, suspicious, afraid of commitment. They do not know it, but they merely model another side of the archetype, the puer, the boy who won't grow up.

Women who have trouble with a dominant father may be attracted to a similar man, or they may be drawn to the puer seemingly to escape the control the father seems to have over their lives. They become the puer's mother, and so re-gain control, but in so doing they have simply become the Father themselves. They wear the pants, even though they do it by mothering their men.

Both men and women seem to have a simple choice: we either become the Father we fear or we continue to avoid him. But our growth requires more: our growth requires that we come face to face with the father. Whatever our father has been, we must accept that. We must accept the real father to know the Divine one.

The real father may have given too much or too little. Ultimately that does not matter. What matters is taking responsibility for our need to have too much or too little. What matters is our own healing. When we say "no" to too much, or "no" to too little, we begin to grow up.

The negative side of the father energy is the tendency to control, dominate, overpower. It is the selfish energy, intent on its own expression, regardless of the needs of others. Strangely enough, this teaches us that we need to have boundaries. The father energy is okay to a point. It is firm, clear, exuberant. It moves with determination through obstacles to its goal. As long as it does not tread on somebody else's toes, it is okay. But when it does, watch out!

A man who runs from the father, or perhaps grows up without one, has a different problem. Raised by women, he becomes fuzzy and confused. He has a poor sense of boundaries. He seeks intimacy, yet he cannot commit to any one woman. He cannot choose. So he keeps the women in his life dangling from the noose of his ambivalence. He cannot give others freedom. He cannot let go. He needs constant attention.

Such a man has not turned to face the father. Behind him where the father lurks, there is empty space and a long wave of hurt. He is afraid to face his pain, for he knows instinctively that, to do so, he must learn to stand alone. He must break his cycle of dependency. He must leave the womb of womanly warmth.

Many men today are in this place. We have left the father for the company of women. We have opened and broadened there. We have learned to talk, to share our feelings. But something is missing. We don't know what we are supposed to do with our lives. We lack aspiration, direction, energy, commitment. Without finding the father, we can't move on. Without finding the father, we can't find ourselves.

Women are also unwhole without the father. In reaction to the father energy, some women have become lesbians or lovers of boys. They have raised their children alone or with other women. Their lovers are puers, often younger, unsure of themselves and their direction in life. A woman tires of such a lover. She wants an equal. But to find an equal, she must face the father energy. To meet a man she cannot control is terrifying. It brings up all the father issues that she buried in her original act of withdrawal.

To face the father is to turn toward someone who knows what he wants and is intent on getting it. That is terrifying to both the woman and the boy. They are afraid that they will be dominated or rejected. But the truth is that the father understands confrontation. Confront the father honestly and with love, and he stands back gratefully. He accepts the correction. He does not want to overstep his bounds. He does not want to dominate. He does not want his wife or his children to withdraw in fear of him.

A society without the father energy is a society that is helpless and wounded. Women and women-dominated men cannot heal the grief that we feel for not finding ourselves or for finding ourselves at the expense of our relationships with men.

We were not brought into this dualistic male-female world to throw out half of the race, half of the ambient energy, half of the Godhead. In spite of our fear, the father remains. And we must reclaim him. We must forgive him for not being there or for being there too much and so forgive ourselves for needing that lesson.

Men are realizing the need to bring the father back into their lives. As they make peace with their real fathers, and as they become fathers to their own children, the healing of the masculine soul begins.

There was a time when God the Father was loved and respected. It was a time of great works of painting, music, and writing. It was a time of celebration. We were held by a strong hand and knew it.

We weren't afraid to test our limits, because we knew those boundaries would hold us safe. But that was a long time ago, a time when men had their rightful place in the world, a time before women had claimed their political and psychological equality.

We must be patient. The pendulum always swings back the other way. And both men and women will benefit from the movement.

As we come to grips with the full meaning of the male archetype, we will come to value a man who is strong, but also gentle, self-directed, but also aware of the needs of others. The father is empowered and knows how to empower. That is his real strength. He has faith in you. He gives you room to make your own mistakes and learn from them. He trusts the truth in you, even as he trusts it in himself.

The vision of God the Father which comes to us through *A Course in Miracles* is the vision that Jesus brought two thousand years ago: A God of love and understanding, a God who knows how to let go, a God who leaves the responsibility for choice with us.

We do not need the vengeful God of the Jews or the Christians anymore. That God was a projection of our fear of our own power. As we accept ourselves with all our mistakes and human frailties, we realize that we do not have to be afraid of that power any more. Indeed, without it, we cannot ascend from darkness.

The journey into the heart is one each of us must make. It is a receptive, feminine journey. It is a journey of being and allowing. Through it we make room for direction to emerge from within. When we come to quiet and complete self-acceptance, the energy of Zeus erupts through us. Then, the ascent to light begins.

Both men and women must come to grips with the father energy to find their purpose in life. To the extent that the purpose of women extends beyond childbearing, they must learn to find the father within and without.

Let us remember that we can reject the form without rejecting the content. We must reject the form of the father that Jesus challenged two thousand years ago. We are long overdue for that. But we must be careful not to banish the father just because we don't like the form of his collective manifestation. Remember, he only manifests that way because that is how we view him in our own minds. As we change our internal relationship to the men in our lives, coming to accept them and embrace them, we will find the collective image changing.

Jesus symbolized the new image of masculine truth. He was gentle, but fearless. He turned the other cheek, but overturned the tables of the money lenders. He was inner directed, but he was not soft. He came from women, but he was not a woman's man.

Women who try to make Jesus "soft" do not understand his great degree of individuation. He was a self-realized man, a man strong in his faith and conviction, a man who was not afraid to challenge authority when necessary.

Yet that Jesus had a gentle, receptive side cannot be denied. He was a man of warmth and tenderness, a man whose heart touched many people. He was approachable, like the God he symbolized. We must not underestimate the importance of this fact. Jesus brought God down to earth. He made God accessible to us in our humanness.

The dogma of the Christian church completely perverts the ontological significance of Jesus. He was not the only Son of God, but the singer of God's praises and presence within the Sonship. He did not claim a special relationship with God, but made God available to all who wanted Him. He brought God to us, and in so doing, helped to bring us to God. That was his role. We were never meant to be dependent on Jesus, for this would undermine our own connection with the divine.

A man who makes others dependent on him does not know how to let go. He does not trust others, and therefore he does not trust himself. Jesus holds us in his love, but only if we call on him. He will not interfere with our freedom to choose.

That is the gift of God the Father, and so it must be the gift of the Son. When we learn to give that gift to each other, we can truly say, as Jesus did, "I and the Father are One." By letting go, we set our brothers and sisters free, claiming responsibility for our own lives. No one can hold us back from our purpose, because we have let go of the chains of co-dependency that bind us.

Without purpose, there can be no joy. For joy is the freedom to be exactly what we are. The father understands this. He supports us in finding our purpose and in expressing our joy.

The father understands the heroic quest for our

own truth. He understands the need to take risks, the need to erect boundaries and cross over them when we are ready, the need to put aside the ideas of others, the need to walk through our fear. He understands the journey to gain the Grail. And he knows that it is not just an outer journey, but also an inner one.

For both men and women, the quest for truth is an essential aspect of our lives. We do not honor ourselves if we do not follow our bliss. Divine Father stands behind the quest, supporting us, encouraging us, giving us a gentle push forward when we feel stuck. He helps us repudiate roles that enslave us to the ideas of others so that we can give birth to our own authentic vision. Through Him we find our right livelihood, our manner of service to the world. And it is in relationship to Him that we confront the issue of supply, financial and otherwise, and address our faith in the nature of the universe to provide for us.

Finding the Father is spiritual work. It is work for both men and women, work that will improve our relationships, by helping us become more individuated. The more deeply we draw from the creative source of our being, the more of ourselves we are able to bring to each other.

We must remember that the phenomenon of co-dependence arises from fear of the father energy, which tears apart all that is inauthentically joined. Relationships that do not honor the Self are challenged by the father. And this challenge is essential for both men and women for, without it, we will be stuck in relationships and roles that limit our creative freedom and encourage conformity and mediocrity.

Meeting Divine Mother

I T IS NOT SURPRISING that, with our poor regard for women in this culture, we find it easier to accept Mother's divine face than her human one. We all want to be nurtured, cared for and accepted just the way we are. This is what Divine Mother offers us: unconditional love and acceptance. Every one of us is Her son or daughter and She loves us all, without exception. However, we are not likely to feel loved in this way until we learn to accept ourselves as we are.

In truth, the Mother archetype has its dark side, and it is this side we must wrestle with in our descent into our psyche. The dark side of the Mother is needy and emotionally controlling. She tries to make us feel guilty because she has sacrificed so much of herself for us. This dark mother dominates her husband and holds her children hostage with the apronstrings of guilt. She cannot let her children go, but seeks to live her own life through them.

Women either emulate or react to such a mother. They marry a weak man they can dominate, or they become submissive to a strong, charismatic male. Either way, their relationship to the feminine principle is negative. The growth of a woman requires that she do more than this. She must learn to face the mother and so come face to face with herself. She must look clearly on her power issues — her need to control or be controlled — and see how they interfere with her ability to give and receive nurturing.

Men too must look at their relationships to the mother. Do they put some women on a pedestal, while treating others as objects? Do they marry a woman who mothers them, or a woman they can dominate and possess? Do they sacrifice their independence for emotional safety? Or do they become caretakers of women who demand more than they can give?

Both women and men must see their mother's strengths and weaknesses clearly and without judgment. Unless they take responsibility for the lessons their mothers bring, they cannot stand in true relationship to the feminine principle.

In our approach to Divine Mother and the other primary women in our lives, we must recognize our lack of love and acceptance of ourselves. As long as we look outside of ourselves for this love and acceptance, we are disappointed. That is Mother's teaching. Mother says "I love you as you are. Learn to love yourself as I love you." Ultimately it is only by learning to "mother" ourselves that we become capable of loving and nurturing others.

Mother teaches us that love lies within, not without. If we want to receive love, we must learn to give it. And to give it, we need to recognize that we have it.

In order to experience love, we must break

through our "conditional" acceptance of ourselves. We must learn to accept ourselves, not just when we feel happy, but when we feel sad, angry, guilty, anxious, worried, or fearful. We must learn the hard lesson that we are not bad, just because we don't feel good.

Genuine love begins here in our existential embrace of ourselves moment to moment. Unless we can love through our pain, we cannot extend our love to others.

It is the Mother principle that forces us to deal with our special relationships. It does this developmentally. It stands with us as we enter into relationships, as we surrender and open our hearts. And it stands with us as these relationships end, comforting us, teaching us gently and patiently that the love we feel is real, but the personality expectations are not.

We must not forget that Divine Mother loves all of her children equally. How then can She teach us to prefer one lover to another? All She can do is help us open our hearts in each relationship, in each situation. All she can do is help us move beyond our preferences, look for love within, and extend love to all the beings in our experience. Mother teaches us to love all, without exception: the poor, the needy, the outcast. They are all dear to Her. By serving them, we serve Her.

Whereas Divine Father asks us to find our individual purpose, Divine Mother asks us to use that purpose, whatever it may be, to serve others. "Learn to take care of yourself," She says, "but once you know how to do that, learn to take care of my children."

She cannot bear to see a single being left in loneliness and despair.

The Mother energy is committed to the collective vision, not the individual one. She is the guardian of the family and the community. Her lessons are lessons of individual restraint and sensitivity to others, sharing, and serving. It is not that She asks us to sacrifice or deny our needs. The father will not allow her to make that request. And, in truth, only the negative side of the goddess makes such a request.

Divine Mother nurtures us until we can stand on our own, until we learn that love is not without, but within our hearts. Then we can leave home and seek wisdom or fortune in the world. But once we have made our fortune or found the wisdom that we seek, Mother bids us return and give back. The life cycle cooperates. Before long, many of us find that we have become mothers or fathers to our own children.

Ready or not, we learn to give back: to our families and to our communities. Mother reminds us that we do not live in isolation, but in relationship with other beings. She reminds us that our journey is an interactive one that does not stop until we are able to embrace all of our brothers and sisters, all of Her children.

The biggest problem with our relationship to the Mother principle is that our development has arrested in the early stages of her process. We have not really learned to love and accept ourselves as we are. We have not learned to find love within. We do not yet understand that love is continuous and eternal and not invested in the objects of relation.

We leave the nest without the emotional tools we need. This is not Mother's fault. It is not even the fault of our birth mothers. It is simply the lesson we came to learn. Because we did not "feel loved" does not mean that Mother did not love us. Feeling loved, we discover, has something to do with learning to accept ourselves moment to moment.

That is why Mother's path is the path of the heart. It is all about love and acceptance of ourselves. We come to this path when we realize through endless mishaps and broken unions that we cannot truly love and serve others until we love and serve ourselves.

When we have begun to master the lessons of self-acceptance, we begin our apprenticeship to the Father. We learn to find our right livelihood and follow our bliss. Mother must be patient. She knows that we must be strong, clear and centered to undertake the work she ultimately has for us. For whatever skills and insights we have gained on our individual quest must ultimately be placed in her service.

Service to others is the continuation of Mother's teaching. Through service, we give back what we have learned. We share our knowledge. We offer our companionship. We learn to nurture others as we have been nurtured.

It must be clear that we cannot follow such a path unless we have first learned to value and take care of ourselves. Giving comes from emotional abundance, not from good intentions. We must be able to be emotionally present in situations that make continual demands on us. We must be able to give all that we have, without feeling that it is not enough. We must trust what we have to give and know that we are just a channel for Mother's love.

Most of all, we must remember that Divine Mother has a human face and we know where we stand with Her only by looking at our relationships with the significant women in our lives. Every man (and woman too) must ask himself a few simple questions: "Do I love and respect the women in my life? Do I forgive my birth mother and accept her as she is now? Do I give back emotionally to my wife or lover?" And if the answer is "no" or "not really," we mustn't despair.

For Mother accepts us where we are. Wherever that is, that is where we begin. If we cannot love others yet, then we start by learning to love ourselves. It is really the same process. But we can't honor it if we try to begin our journey on terrain we aren't ready to handle. It may seem that we are going backwards when we retrace our steps to the foot of the mountain. But in reality we will save time if we begin our climb with the proper gear and supplies.

We need to remember: "there is always a place where forgiveness is relevant in my life." When things get difficult or confused, this is where we must begin our healing. "Whatever seems to be happening in my life, I am okay as I am. I am acceptable as I am. I am worthy of love. I am willing to be loving and gentle with myself right now." That is Divine Mother's message to us. It is her hymn of praise.

Embracing the
Inner Partner

TO BE ANDROGYNOUS does not mean to be asexual, but to be composed of male and female elements. There are as many images of androgyny as there are people. Each person represents a unique combination of male and female physical and psychological aspects.

The task of accepting ourselves requires that we embrace all sides of our nature. Merely to accept our bodily being in its male or female form is not enough. Merely to accept our intellectual attributes without accepting our emotional temperament and sensuality falls short of wholeness.

To self-actualize, I must come to terms with the fact that I am a unique man or woman. To be sure, I cannot do this in isolation. I see myself in perpetual relationship with other men and women.

The problem is not the fact that I stand in relation to others, but my need to measure myself against others, my need for their approval. That need interrupts and perverts my primary, existential task of coming to accept myself as I am.

When I feel inadequate or shamed because I do not measure up to others, or when I feel entitled because

I measure up well, power issues emerge. Lessons begin to manifest early in my childhood in my relationship to father and mother and siblings. Later, I seek to work my power issues out in the context of my intimate relationships, where I feel safe and accepted enough to explore and work through old trauma.

Power lessons are twofold in their manifestation: either I try to empower myself by dominating/controlling others or by allowing myself to be dominated/controlled by someone whom I think has my best interests at heart. I am either the victim or the perpetrator, or perhaps I am both in different situations. Neither role helps me discover my authentic power.

To empower myself, I must accept myself and learn to trust in my own life. To empower others I must accept them as they are and trust that they will find their own path into the light.

If I try to carry others, I will tire quickly and be unable to complete my own journey. If I allow myself to be carried, I may find myself moving in an inappropriate direction; often an easy ride becomes a hard one when I find I have to re-trace my steps.

Honoring myself and honoring others are different tasks. Yet whenever I do one successfully, I make it easier for myself to do the other. I can't cross over boundaries until I have first learned to respect them.

Tearing down the walls of fear never works. It simply invokes more fear. If I want to cross over the sense of separation I feel from you, I must be willing to meet you half way, but never further. For that is a trespass; that is an attack.

To feel compassion for you, I must keep my distance until you invite me in. I must be willing to wait until you are ready. I cannot give my gift until you ask for it. Your manner of asking can be subtle or overt. But I must not offer myself to you until I hear your call for love.

Giving people space is one of the greatest gifts we can give. It's a way of saying "I trust you." And when I trust you, it's easier for you to trust yourself.

To come to true acceptance of myself, I must be willing to explore the full range of my thoughts, feelings and experiences. I must come to hold all that I am in a gentle embrace: my desires, fears, expectations, dreams, aspirations and fantasies. I become more authentic as I give myself permission to think what I think, do what I do, and feel what I feel. I stop censoring who I am. And I also allow others to be what they are without trying to control their thoughts, feelings, and actions. This is not so easy a task. If you think it is, try it for a while. I guarantee you that it will be a sobering experience.

We just do not realize the depth or degree of control we place on ourselves and the other people in our lives.

All efforts to control what happens in our lives are fear-based. That does not mean that they are bad. Making our tendency to control "bad" just deepens our fear. All we can do about our need to control is learn to see it and accept it.

When you accept your need to control, it no longer has any charge on it. You see it for what it is. When any aspect of our darkness is seen and is accepted, it is brought into the sacred place, the place empty of judgment, the place of existential affirmation. That is the place where fear dissolves and darkness disappears in the light. It is the place where the wounded child is befriended and blessed.

The connection between acceptance and love is so profound, it is surprising that it has not been emphasized more. In acceptance lies the spiritual affirmation of the inherent goodness of all things. No matter what the apparent flaw or lack, when it is accepted, it is transformed into a key that opens the door of the heart.

Allowing ourselves to be is a surrender to who we are. We do this out of the recognition that we do not know who we are, that in a sense the more we do, the more we think, the less we know.

To live our lives without the compulsion to think or to do, is to allow whatever is there to blossom of its own accord. What is there when I remove the shell of thought? What is there when the circumstance of all my doings dissolves?

If we want the real stuff, this is where we find it. Everything else is an overlay. It is the meaning "we" give to what is beyond definition.

And so we ask: "what happens if I don't move compulsively into this relationship just because it is available and I am lonely? What if I stay with the loneliness and with the relationship too? What if I don't try to use the relationship to fix the loneliness?

What if I allow myself to live organically and with trust, day to day, honoring the people I meet, but not looking to them to meet my needs? What happens when I am content to be and to wait, when I listen for a deep mutuality in my relationships and allow myself to feel the sadness if it doesn't come when or how I want it to be?

What happens if I allow myself to move through that deep judgmental feeling that there is something wrong with me because I'm not with a partner? What will I learn about my male or female nature when I surrender to the flow of my life, wherever it leads?"

These questions take courage to ask. They call upon my wholeness. They call on my willingness to trust myself. They call upon my willingness to trust in my relatedness to other men and women. They suggest that something wonderful and instructive can happen in my life without my making it happen. And they suggest that what happens can be experienced without judgment, for its meaning lies beyond my ability to judge or compare.

As a man, I am attracted to women. Women symbolize some aspect of my inner nature which I need to embrace. The woman in my life offers me the opportunity to find the feminine within. I, in turn, offer my partner the opportunity to discover the masculine presence within. This can only be a mutual experience. It is a gift that we give each other when we both stop trying to mold the relationship to meet our separate needs.

Joining together as men and women thus becomes a powerful metaphor for uniting the Father and Mother energies in our own souls. Yet we do not have to be with a partner to be in relationship to the male and female archetypes. In our aloneness, in our waiting and wanting, we are preparing a place for a new intimacy to begin.

In order to find a partner to be well with, to love well with, and to dance well with, I need to attend to the sacred space within. A man is brought to his partner through his relationship with Divine Mother, or the invisible feminine that lies in his heart. So too, a woman is brought to her mate through her inner relationship with the Father.

If we want to know who our Divine parents are, we must learn to listen to their voices in our grief as well as in our joy. For truly, our intimacy with others comes through our intimacy with our inner partner. The outer relationship that opens gracefully before us is just a reflection of the divine synergy within.

PART SEVEN

Relationship: The Divine Dance

"We come together
that we may move more
deeply into ourselves.
And we move apart
that we may come
together again. In that
dance, there is stillness.
In that joining, there
is that which has
never been apart."

———————•———————

Relationship: The Divine Dance

Breaking the Cycle of Co-Dependency

M Y FRIEND CHANTAL (not her real name) has a pattern of being attracted into relationships with men who are not free to make a commitment to her. Recently, she got involved with Greg, who pursued her vigorously, even though he was still involved with Jessica.

Greg told Chantal that he had wanted to end his relationship with Jessica for some time, and his involvement with Chantal gave him the opportunity to do just that. While Greg tried to come to closure with Jessica, he was unable to do so. So once again, my friend found herself in a relationship that did not honor her need for intimacy and commitment.

It is likely that Chantal herself was afraid of intimacy and commitment and these men just mirrored that fact back to her. It is also likely that attracting these uncommitted men into her life gave her the perfect lesson: the opportunity to stand up for herself and refuse a relationship that compromised her integrity.

Accepting half a relationship when she wanted a whole one was masochistic and self-defeating. It was just a way of punishing herself. Her biggest lesson was simply to wake up to this fact.

Greg wanted to keep seeing Chantal and Jessica. It was hard for Chantal to say no, because she did not want to lose Greg. It was hard for Jessica to say no for the same reason. Greg couldn't choose, because he was afraid of commitment, and Chantal and Jessica couldn't choose because they were afraid to be alone.

Chantal was feeling powerless, but she was fully capable of choosing the reality she wanted. In order to do, however, so she needed to say "no" to Greg's insidious attempt to manipulate her into meeting his needs. In her case, saying no was a tremendous act of affirmation of her own being.

In thinking this situation through, Chantal remembered that she had recently turned down a job because the pay was not enough. The guy who wanted to hire her did his best to convince her to take the job, but she flatly refused. "I won't work for that," she told him.

She began to realize that she needed to deliver the same message to Greg: "I won't accept a relationship that lacks mutual commitment. I deserve more than that." Chantal needed to affirm herself. She needed to refuse to accept less than her heart's desire.

To say no to manipulation, is to say yes to self-trust and the flow of grace. It is to refuse to be molded into someone else's idea of the way things should be. It is a movement into our own depth. It forces us to find our own direction and stick with it.

We are all afraid to do this, because it often means leaving others behind. It means saying to others: "follow your heart; don't follow me. If your path runs alongside mine, we can travel together, but that is a decision that each of us must make and take responsibility for. I am not responsible for your choice, nor are you for mine."

It may seem that this arrangement offers little security but, in truth, no other arrangement offers any more. Certainly other arrangements promise more, but do they deliver? People make all kinds of plans to be together, yet only stay together as long as their ego needs are being met by a relationship.

As we all know, this doesn't happen for very long. As soon as romance dwindles, ego conflicts start. And then the real test comes. Do the partners in this relationship aspire to use their experience together to grow? Are they growth partners or fantasy partners? Are they willing to look at each other face to face, or do they prefer to hide behind the masks of mutual expectation and denial?

Relationships that pierce the veil of fantasy become lifelong friendships rooted in the soil of mutual understanding and support. They cease to be concerned with getting or doing. They become a simple experience of being together.

Whether alone or with another, we cannot escape the existential ground of being. Life is not fireworks, but a gentle flow back to God. In that flow we learn to forgive ourselves and others. We learn to forgive the world. And we learn to forgive our heroes for not rescuing us. In that flow, each one of us becomes a quiet hero, simply by doing our best and knowing that it is enough.

If I think that you have something that I need, then I do not know who I am. I have not learned to trust myself yet. That trust is the essence of my relatedness to life. Without it I can have many relationships, but they will be exploitive ones.

It is absurd to think that I can love you if I don't trust my own relatedness to life. I can't find that relatedness through you or anyone else. It is part of my existential embrace of my life. It is part of my "yes" to life.

To make my "yes" conditional upon your acceptance of me is not only unwise; it is emotionally destructive for both of us. My "yes" must be said on its own terms. It is worked out in my relationship with myself and my relationship with God.

And this working out takes place every moment and every day of my life. It is a continual dialogue with God. To try to replace my dialogue with God with my dialogue with you places unnecessary pressure on our relationship.

I do not always love you unconditionally, nor do you love me always in this way. But God loves you and I always without conditions. And my sanity and yours lies in waking up to this fact. If I can help you remember that, then I have helped you. But if I would rather that you hear my voice than His, then I have stood in your light and cast a shadow upon you.

It is not my job to say "yes" for you. It is not your

job to say "yes" for me. Each of us must move in the direction in which we perceive the light. Any interference in this movement is manipulative. It is simply a form of attack.

My task in this life is to honor myself. If I can do that, I stand a good chance of honoring you too. For honoring you and honoring myself are the same. In seeking to make you responsible for my life, I establish my own guilt. In releasing you from all responsibility for how I think and feel, I grant myself the freedom to make a better choice.

No matter how many corners I back into, I can always find the middle of the ring. I have only to be completely honest and completely defenseless.

No one can take my freedom of choice away. For in that freedom lies the key to my innocence and yours.

The Dance of
Distance and Closeness

BEING AWAY from those we love always helps us appreciate them more. We remember the important things about our relationships and put the little things that annoy us aside. We remember our purpose in being together and embrace it again.

The same thing happens when people we care about die. We remember the good things about them and about our interactions with them. Or if there are major issues of abuse in our relationships with these people, we realize that the time has come to forgive. With their death, we understand that we have a choice as to whether we want to continue to live with the blame and the shame.

In a Death Lodge, the native American Indian spends the last hours before his transition out of the body putting his relationships with others right. Spouse, parents, children, friends come to visit him and to say good-bye. This ritual is one of purification. He does not want to leave with unfinished business.

Participants in twelve step programs are encouraged to make amends to those persons who have been hurt by their behavior. In order to move ahead, to move out of addiction and the shame-based patterns that caused it, one must learn how to forgive oneself and how to make peace with one's people.

We must face the fact that we are not a nation or society of peacemakers. Making peace with ourselves and others is something we have to learn how to do. Somewhere deep within we know that we are innocent, but we do not remember how to get there. We cannot see through the stain, the sin, the shame and blame.

Vision quest rituals are essential for the spiritual journey. They help us leave behind our daily routine and habitual thought patterns. They help us rediscover our innocence. They help us find authentic guidance and direction. Each of us returns from the quest with a new direction that is essential to transforming the negative, restrictive patterns of our lives.

Before we can return home as light bearers we must find the light in the darkness of our souls. We must face our fears, cross over our own self-erected boundaries. A society that does not value this subterranean quest will not reach its creative potential. Individuals who do not value it will remain stuck in patterns of co-dependency and abuse.

The Self is not a known territory, but a wilderness. Too often we forget that. Too often we reach the boundaries of what we know about ourselves and turn back.

Before we can venture out on the quest, we must say good-bye to our people. We must put things right and be clear that we are not running away, but moving to take the next step in our lives.

The quest must not become an excuse to avoid intimacy or commitment. It must be a movement beyond complacency.

Good relationships are both nurturing and challenging. They provide support and encouragement and they motivate us to take new risks in our lives. This represents a balance of the masculine and feminine aspects within each individual and each relationship.

Relationships become restrictive or abusive when there is an imbalance of polar forces in the individual or in the relationship. When the masculine energy (in either woman or man) is prevented from moving outward and exploring new ground, it rebounds inward with a vengeance. The hearth cannot function as a hearth unless one comes and goes to it voluntarily. On the other hand, when the feminine energy (in either man or woman) is prevented from nurturing self and other, the hearth is compromised and any attempt to do things outwardly is undermined by weakness and lack of resolve from within.

For the opposites to dance, they must yield to one another. Rigidity on either end means a tendency toward stasis and inflexibility.

A man who can be gentle and nurturing and a woman who can be clear and assertive together stake out new ground for themselves and for their relationship. The goal is not to reverse roles, but to loosen the grip of roles upon each partner. This allows for energy, spontaneity, and a deepening of trust.

The rituals of self-exploration help us see our relationships with new eyes. They help us put aside our petty differences, overcome our rusty images of self and other, and bring an emotional conviction back into our relationships. Our desire energy is rekindled and fuels the relationship, helping it move to new ground.

By contrast, people who do not spend time honoring their individual guidance and growth needs do not tolerate times of aloneness. In their need to control and make the relationship predictable, they suffocate one another with demands and expectations. They are jealous, insecure, afraid to be alone, and easily threatened. They are like a caterpillar suffocating inside its cocoon, because it is afraid to crawl out.

Unless we emerge, however ungainfully, from the prison of our own fearful self-image, we cannot grow our wings. The butterfly does not emerge without squirming. Indeed, it might be said that squirming is just training for the time when he will have to learn to move his wings.

Each of us must learn continually to shed the old skin of persona to meet the emerging lineaments of self. Like it or not, we are always in the process of giving birth to ourselves.

To be sure, it is not easy to find a partner committed to the transformational journey. But we always meet someone who mirrors back to us the degree of independence we are ready to claim for ourselves. To seek to change our partners is thus an impossible task. Instead, we must give *ourselves* permission to grow.

Nobody can force us to take risks we are not ready to take. So, if we are not ready to cross the bridge where our fear runs wide and deep, let us walk by the river until we find a place to cross that does not frighten us.

Your partner, the man or woman who walks with you, is just as afraid as you are. You may not be afraid of the same things, but your fear level is equivalent. That is one reason you can walk together.

Think about it. Would you walk with one who had no fear or one who had far more fear than you? One would scare the daylights out of you; the other would bore you to tears.

As each of us moves through our fear, we think that we are going somewhere. But that is just the illusion of the journey. The journey is not one of going or becoming; it is one of self-discovery. Everything we need already exists within. Understanding this in one's heart and mind is the fulfillment of the promise of this incarnation. It is the awakening to the Christ energy in ourselves and others.

Making the choice for love, moment to moment, offers us an intimation of the place where separation ends. That place is within each of us, yet we approach it together. It is in the midst of us, yet we must inquire of it each of us within our own hearts.

We come together that we may move more deeply into ourselves. And we move apart that we may come together again. In that dance, there is stillness. In that joining, there is that which has never been apart.

Awakening Together

EVERY TIME I TRY to make someone or something special in my life I give it the power to injure me. I invest it with meaning that it does not have of itself.

When you are attracted to me, I am not satisfied with your ever-so-tentative proximity. I am not happy that you buzz around me like a bee tasting the nectar of a new flower. I want to hold you, so that I know that you will be there for me.

So I call you my lover, my partner, or my soulmate. I anchor the relationship in time and space. I make it part of my practical, day to day world. I schedule you in to my life.

By giving the relationship a name and a purpose, I remove its mystery. I move it from unknown to known, from unpredictable to predictable. I take a relationship which has a certain spiritual presence and fit it out with roles and expectations. I take something which is alive in the moment and consign it to the past. I build a defensive barrier against the energy the relationship engenders so that I can be sure I won't be hurt.

I decide what the relationship means based on

an inner sense of lack. I assume that the relationship is here to make things better in my life, to bring me the companionship and support I so desperately want and need. I never assume that the relationship comes to unsettle the areas of my life that are rigid and unyielding. I never assume that the purpose of the relationship is to wake me up.

My definition of the relationship never comes close to its truth, because that truth can only emerge as my partner and I live our lives. The meaning of our union reveals itself spontaneously as our relationship evolves. Yet as soon as mutuality is lost, so is the meaning of the relationship. All that remains then is the ego's meaning, the thin shell of self-imposed definition that cracks as soon emotions well up.

Some ten years ago, I was developing a new system of divination that synthesized some of the principles of the I Ching and the Egyptian Tarot. Each number had a corresponding image. For number twenty one, which represented spiritual union, the artist and I chose the image of interlocking rings. To us, this image meant a relationship between two people who were whole inside themselves, yet also interdependent. As I have thought about this image during the last ten years, I have come to the conclusion that it is not a totally accurate one.

The interlocking rings suggest the inability to move in and out of relationship. The image is static and therefore not accurate. A better image is of two circles touching. Their coming together is voluntary and mutual. Each can step back or step forward. The step back represents withdrawal in fear. The step forward represents inappropriate crossing of boundaries into co-dependency.

The dance of relatedness involves both the forward and backward movement toward and away from boundaries. While it is not healthy for boundaries to be crossed, neither is it appropriate for boundaries to be the cause for withdrawal from intimacy. The truth is, however, that boundaries will be crossed and they will be used to justify separation. This is inevitable. Without trespassing and withdrawing in fear, we would not learn the lessons of mutual acceptance and forgiveness, which are the basis of genuine intimacy.

To discover our essential spiritual relatedness, we need to make mistakes and work through our inappropriate ideas about relationships. We need to learn to be with our fear without running away, and to be with our desire without grasping. We need to learn to join the dance and dance the joining. It is a continual process of give and take, which only pushes our buttons when we stop listening and learning from it.

Two circles touch at a single point, and that point becomes the center of a new circle symbolizing the relationship itself. This is the point where two join together as one. It is where the Holy Spirit enters or where the Spirit of God dwells. It is a place that is neither outside nor inside, but between us. Its home is not in a body or in a separate mind, but in a relationship.

In the place where minds join, there are no boundaries. There is no you and me. Your interests and mine are not different. There is a single purpose. This is not a place that we can get to by appropriating each other emotionally or physically. It is not a place won by aggression of any kind. It is a place that exists within the boundaries themselves. To explore this place means to touch without appropriating or recoiling; it is to be present in the moment with equal regard for self and other. It is not an esoteric place, but an obvious place we rush over in our hurry to separate or join.

This is the spiritual frontier. It is the wilderness that partners face together as they come to true mutuality. It is the place where the definitions of self and other begin to blur precisely because they have been respected up to that point. This is not a merging of one into another, but a mutual discovery of the *a priori* relatedness that runs like a silver thread through all relationships. It is a surrender to the deepest aspect of Reality, where each self becomes Self, where Atman and Brahman merge.

I cannot find this frontier if I am preoccupied with myself or my own spiritual growth. I cannot find it if I am preoccupied with you. I can find it only when I come to accept myself and you existentially, as we are in any moment in time, without needing to define who we are as individuals or as a couple.

I come to this frontier by being myself and allowing you to be yourself. I come with you, not because of you or in spite of you. I come by trusting the journey, and not by needing to know where it leads me. I come by trusting you, even when I do not know whether we are still walking together.

In truth you live outside all of my images of you. You live outside even your own images of self. Your energy and consciousness animate your body, but you are not that body. Thoughts and emotions move through your mind, but you are not those thoughts or emotions. Who you are is much deeper than that. It is much broader than that. It simply cannot be defined or confined.

When I allow you to be that deep and broad, that undefined, I see only God in you. When I allow myself to be that unlimited, I see only God in myself. This is the frontier. This is the place we came to explore.

Gradually, I begin to see that I am the only one who limits myself and my relationships. All external limits are just reflections of my own fear of who I am or who you are.

I make myself small, because that seems easier to deal with. I make our relationship small, because it becomes manageable to me. Biting off a small piece doesn't raise my fear level. The problem, of course, is that I grow beyond that level and so do you. The old limits must come down as we expand. The old definitions must give way to less rigid ones.

All of this suggests a developmental process. That is what moving through our fear means. As we move through our fear, we cast aside our self-imposed restrictions. That seems to be a real process to us, and psychologically it is. But none of these defenses that we have built against love has any existential reality. Only love itself has that reality. Everything else is a matter of perception.

And, as we know, perceptions change.

Love remains constant beneath all of the permutations of belief. The limits we place on love are not real, but we believe that they are. That belief creates a psychological world, a world of perception, which we inhabit. As each self-imposed belief is dismantled, we awaken to the love and free flow of energy that exists beneath it. As we release the "world of our perceptions," we awaken to a world we did not make, a world of beauty and mystery.

In that world we are all equal. One relationship is no more important or valuable than another. Everyone is accepted and loved equally. Everyone touches with mutual respect. There is no attack, no violation.

That world is familiar to each one of us. As we awaken to it, it feels that we are coming home. We know this place, from deep within. It is not just some fantasy, some idealistic vision. It is who we are. It is where we began our journey.

When we were here we knew. When we left this place, we began to forget. And all that transpired in between was a tale of forgetfulness and remembering.

Let us be grateful to each other for the mirror of every relationship we have had. Each has accelerated our remembrance. Each has brought us face to face within, and without. Now heaven and hell are joined in a single place, and from it emanates a steady heartbeat. From far away, you can hear it, like a drum beating. From far out in the forest, you can hear the song of the drum and follow its footsteps home.

Challenges to Our Freedom

"Our guilt tells us
that beauty does not lie
within us, but only in
others. It tells us that
we better listen to the
teacher who plays to
our unhappiness
and invalidates our
experience ... It's hard
to believe that right now
we hold the key to our
own enlightenment and
that key is forgiveness."

Challenges to Our Freedom

External Authority

RECENTLY I MET a group of people who were students of *A Course in Miracles* and members of a community in the mid-west. These people had surrendered to a teacher who called himself "master."

This "master" said that *A Course in Miracles* was literally true and that by following its teachings one could undergo a physical transformation — which he likened to the resurrection of Jesus — and escape the world. He claimed to have done this himself and to have come back to help us do the same. In his community, members were encouraged to let go of their attachment to their ego-identities and their entire past experience. They could then become "of one mind," and experience God directly.

While the ecstatic experiences of community members seemed legitimate, their passivity in relationship to their "master" was alarming. They did not question any of his teachings and looked upon such questioning as fearful and a form of attack against the "master." This encouraged an attitude of blind obedience to authority on the part of community members. Leaders on the other hand exhibited distrust, if not outright paranoia, when challenged to describe their ideas in an open forum. "The only way you can understand this," outsiders were told, "is if you come here and experience it."

Those who bought this reasoning went to visit the community. Many of them were impressed by their energetic experiences and any objections they might have had were washed away in the fervor to surrender to the master's teaching. Some decided to sell their belongings and join the community. A few who continued to question were told they were resisting and encouraged to leave. Meanwhile, outsiders could get little information about what went on in the community.

The situation was set up perfectly to keep critics away, and to keep in the community only those members who were willing to surrender to the group norms. It was a classic environment for mind control and manipulation. Thus, even if the teachings of the "master" were enlightening and the experiences of community members were ecstatic, the structure was still set up for abuse. In addition, teachers from the community exhibited the attitude that "we have the way and you don't; we have the real *A Course in Miracles* experience; the rest of you are just wasting your time." They tended to put down people outside their community, and played to the unhappiness of potential members by promising them a more ecstatic experience.

Clearly this phenomenon has happened many times in many religious contexts. I guess we should not be surprised that it has happened under the banner of *A Course in Miracles*. In spite of the Course's clear emphasis on inner authority, some of us have been seduced by the "old world" claims of an authority that lies outside our own experience.

This old world solution to our spiritual crisis offers us a guru or master, a dogmatic teaching, and a quintessential experience. For students who are impatient with the gradual process of undoing, the promise of a sudden awakening, or one that can happen in a few months in a supportive community, seems very appealing.

It's also seductive to think that a "master teacher" could be available to us here. "What if Jesus were here and we missed the opportunity to learn from Him?" That type of thinking —and we all have it — just fosters the tendency to look outside of ourselves for answers.

We must see this tendency to look for a savior outside of ourselves for what it is...another call for a special relationship. We want a special teacher, a special teaching, and a special experience. Then we are ready to believe. Of course, our belief in specialness gives us exactly what we ask for. Unfortunately, it is not the answer to our problems, but yet another test of our willingness to trust the holiness within.

In my opinion *A Course in Miracles* is a radical teaching precisely because it does away with the need for intermediaries or religious hierarchies. A Course that tells us plainly that the answer to our problems lies in our own minds is difficult to exploit or tamper with. The problem is that we have trouble believing this. We are not willing to trust our innocence or explore our equality. Our guilt runs very deep.

Our guilt tells us that beauty does not lie within us, but only in others. It tells us that we better listen to the teacher who plays to our unhappiness and invalidates our experience because he's probably right about us. We've always known there was something missing in our spiritual practice, and now we know what it is!

We find it easier to hear this message than the message that we have everything we need right now. It's hard to believe that we have an inner teacher who has perfect understanding. It's hard to believe that right now we hold the key to our own enlightenment and that key is forgiveness. It's hard to see the illusion the ego creates with compassion for ourselves and others.

Yet that is what this process is all about. Without developing this deeply rooted compassion for one another, ecstatic experience simply becomes another addiction, another block to our awareness of love's presence. With it, however, our joy manifests in rituals of inclusion that dissolve the perceived barriers of separation between us.

In the final analysis, it does not matter whether I agree with my brother. But it does matter that I love him. For, lest I love him, my disagreement with him is but an attack. And then it means nothing. But if I love him, my fidelity to my own inner truth becomes a lifeline for both of us.

I cannot affirm myself by rejecting my brother. Nor can I affirm my brother by denying my own experience. I must remain faithful both to him and to myself.

The End
of Specialness

SPECIALNESS ENDS when I stop putting myself down and looking up to you, or when I stop over-valuing myself and undervaluing you. It doesn't matter what form specialness takes. The forms are endless. And we have seen that there is no essential difference between special love and special hate.

The search for a teacher, a belief system, or an ecstatic experience can be one of specialness. Then "I have something that you don't have," or "we have something that they don't have." The truth is that whatever we have that isn't shared simply represents the ego's need for reinforcement. It shows our deep-seated insecurity and need for approval.

The ego's beliefs will always be riddled by insecurity, because they are based upon separation. Feeling separate, the ego needs the agreement of others. Yet, no matter how much agreement it receives, it seeks more. A single person who disagrees can drive it mad.

Spirit, on the other hand, needs no reinforcement. It feels joined with others even when there is disagreement. It is able to love and accept others exactly as they are, for it knows only how to bless. Its security comes from the fact that it trusts itself and so extends that trust to others.

The end of specialness comes when we truly understand that what we give we receive, or as the Course puts it "everything I give I give to myself." Every time I affirm you, I also affirm myself. But I must also understand that it is impossible for me to affirm you if I haven't also affirmed myself. My affirmation of you cannot be at the expense of myself or it has no meaning. If I do not love myself, I cannot love you. My love for you can only deepen the love I already feel for myself. I do not have to become empty to receive from you, nor do you have to become empty to receive from me. That is the old myth of teaching and learning. The new myth says teachers are learners and vice versa. The only way I can give or receive from you is to recognize that what dwells in me also dwells in you. Only in that mutual recognition can true learning take place, for all learning is mutual.

The end of specialness means a totally new and exciting exploration of our equality. It is an experiment in trust. I don't believe that we have begun to move fully into this arena. For the old myth beckons, offering us teachings and teachers who hold us hostage to our insecurity and our fear. Our guilt prevails over our trust, over our memory of our innocence.

Yet, it is clear to me that this is the direction *A Course in Miracles* asks us to take. It is a movement into community as equals. We will struggle with that, but if our commitment is deep enough, we will find a way. Before our mutual practice of forgiveness, no obstacles can stand. I have seen the truth of this more than once.

Capitulation
Versus Surrender

I N MY PRACTICE of The Course I am clear that
the process of individuation is not at odds with
the process of surrender.

Indeed, they are dual aspects of the same process. The more secure I am within myself, the easier
it is for me to let go of beliefs that no longer work for
me and open myself up to new ideas and experiences.

When I surrender, however, I do so to Spirit, not
to you, no matter how wise you may be; nor do I ask
you to surrender to me. For we are equals and we are
here to work through our illusory belief that any one
of us has anything the other does not have.

My resistances and defense mechanisms dissolve when I am ready to let them go. Love melts
away fear. It does not batter it down.

As I come to peace within, I come to peace with
you. It cannot happen otherwise. My peace with you
cannot be won by capitulations to your demands or
surrender to your wisdom, or vice versa.

The cycle of projection stops when I no longer
need to use you to justify anything in my life. It stops
when I accept both you and myself, without needing
to change either one of us. That is our existential

greeting to each other as brother and sister. That is our Namaste, our bow to the divinity in one another.

False joining happens when I want you to be like me or vice versa. Such joining is always threatened by difference, by questioning, because it maintains itself only by agreement.

Real joining has nothing to do with agreement. It has nothing to do with surrender to group mind. Real joining is based on my unconditional acceptance of your innocence and my own.

You do not have to agree with me for me to love you. Love that demands agreement is not love but control. It is the ego's version of joining. It does not trust others to find their own way. It cannot give them the space to make their own mistakes. It pushes and it prods. It demands, expects, and retaliates when its expectations go unmet.

Cults, cliques, and all exclusive groupings ask individual members to give their allegiance to some idea and/or personality outside themselves. This is the ultimate special relationship. You may call it surrender, but it is really attack. Giving anyone permission to make decisions for you not only robs you of your own creative freedom, it also reinforces the guilt of the one who would decide for you.

As your brother, I cannot decide for you. If you come to me in search of answers, I can only share my experience and urge you to remain faithful to your own. The answers you need are already present in your mind and in your life. You do not have to go to a special place to find them. Your real teacher is with you wherever you are.

Any teaching that asks me to deny my life is a teaching of escape. It cannot but be based on fear. Jesus does not ask me to deny the body or the world. He just asks me to see them rightly. Those who insist that freedom cannot be found until we leave the body and the world behind miss the point. Rejecting the physical world simply makes it special, in the same way that being attached to it does.

To move beyond duality in our spiritual practice, we must find a way to accept things as they are. This is the basis of unity thinking. It is also the foundation for all ecstatic experience. My surrender to my life exactly as it is in the moment brings me face to face with God, for it is an acknowledgment of spiritual perfection.

When I accept my life, I learn to see everything with the eyes of love. What I needed to judge before, whether in myself or you, I now see differently. What I sought to bind, I learn to set free, and what I sought to escape from, I now welcome with open arms. Ultimately, every fear I have is a fear of my own power. Once I accept that power and take responsibility for using it lovingly, my need to find fault with you or with my own life diminishes greatly.

Recognizing Boundaries and Moving Beyond Them

WHEN WE IGNORE the need for boundaries, we attack. When we lovingly respect those boundaries, we create the mutual trust necessary to go beyond them.

We cannot force each other to grow. We cannot brow beat each other with the truth. When my brother or sister is fearful of my approach, do I keep coming? On the contrary, I say "I see that this makes you fearful. Sorry." And I withdraw. That act of understanding and compassion places the whole event in the hands of the Holy Spirit. I must not be invested in the timing or question the final outcome. I know that my sister will be healed when she is ready. And I know that my own healing depends on my willingness to allow her whatever time she needs.

Our ability to respect our differences actually makes joining possible. It enables us to look beyond those differences into each other's hearts. On the other hand, our refusal to accept our differences places us on a collision course in which our egos struggle for dominance. Joining is sought through force, an impossible task!

Our willingness to accept each other as we are

results in great diversity. That is the essence of the democratic impulse.

Toward that end information sharing, discussion, even controversy are helpful. Good questions support joining. Pat answers do not. Although at a profound level I think that there is only one question and one answer, clearly we ask that question differently and we come to the answer in our own way. In fact, I honestly believe that if you took away the uniqueness of the process, the fact that the answer is a universal one would have no meaning.

Without the integrity of the search, the goal is meaningless. And to those who would give us the goal without the process, I say it is an empty promise. Each of us must go as we are, from the place where we begin. We have only our own experience, and it cannot be discounted, although in it suffering and joy commingle.

Our task is not to seize the joy or make the suffering go away, but to be with each as it comes, to look without judgment, to see and come to understand. Easy answers will always be offered, but they do not bring us peace. They simply take us away from the process of observation. In the end, we will come back to it, for it is the only way that we can learn to be free of judgment.

It is not easy to use the mind to understand the mind, yet that is what we must do. We must see the consequences of our thoughts. We must have the experiences dictated by our beliefs. That is what this world is. It is our creation moment to moment.

And only as we come to understand it moment

to moment do we develop the ability to transcend the limitations of our own conceptual mind. That is the process.

In truth, we can only speak of the process. Whatever we say about the goal will be misunderstood, because it can only be understood in relation to our process, and our process is always unique. In pursuit of the goal, we try to make our process conform to that of another who seems to be more advanced than us, but this only distracts us from our own path. For this journey, whatever it is for you or me — and rest assured it is different for each of us — there is no substitute. Right now, right here, at the precise speed I am traveling, I have exactly the conditions I need for my enlightenment. If I accept the tools for learning that exist in my life, I cannot but learn, and learn I do, but at my own pace. Let me measure my progress against yours and I will confuse both of us.

All this has to do with understanding boundaries. Too often we interfere with each other, because we are insecure about our own direction. That, I suppose, is inevitable. But we must learn to see it; we must look clearly at the result of our trespasses against each other. We must understand that every resistance we have to our organic life process is a result of fear of who we are. We simply do not trust ourselves, and that of course is why we do not trust each other.

No amount of manipulation is going to bring me to my goal of peace. I come to peace by being peaceful. The process itself becomes the goal, and so the goal is achieved of itself. I do not come to peace by trying to change myself, nor do I come to peace by trying to change you. Peace comes when I know I am okay as I am right now, and so are you.

Recognizing boundaries is simply the remembrance of this fact. If I think I have to change to get your approval, I get anxious. Old fears arise that I am not worthy. If I think that I have to change you in order to be happy, I become neurotically invested in your behavior. When you don't support me overtly, I feel betrayed.

My lack of boundaries leads toward judgment and projection, and not away from them. This is "false joining." It lasts only as long as both people agree on sacrifice. Beyond that point, the fear and the anger erupt with a vengeance.

On the other hand, when we confront our differences honestly and head on, we set each other free. We recognize that we are joined together at a deeper level than words or even deeds. I do not have to agree with you. You do not have to meet with my approval. That is our existential affirmation of one another. And every time I see you in this way, I affirm my own freedom to be as I choose to be.

This is the greatest gift I can give you: my trust, indeed my certainty that you will do what's best for you. I can do this only if I see the face of Christ in you and in myself equally.

PART NINE

Words to the Wise

"No amount of manipulation is going to bring me to my goal of peace. I come to peace by being peaceful. The process itself becomes the goal, and so the goal is achieved of itself."

———————•———————

Words to the Wise

The Practice of Acceptance

I F YOU DON'T ACCEPT all of your experience, how can you come to wholeness? How can you embrace your life?

Acceptance happens with understanding, but understanding cannot come so long as you resist or deny your experience. Indeed the more you resist your experience, the less meaning it will have for you. To understand, you must first accept. You will come to know your purpose to the extent that you are willing to work with your life exactly as it is.

Your life is your spiritual path. Don't be quick to abandon it for promises of bigger and better experiences. You are getting exactly the experiences you need to grow. If your growth seems too slow or uneventful for you, it is because you have not fully embraced the situations and relationships at hand. The more you practice acceptance, the more quickly you move through your lessons.

As you begin to accept your life as it is, it will be easier for you to accept the lives of others. This is the appropriate extension of the practice. It is no more appropriate for you to judge or seek to change another's life than it is to judge or seek to change your own.

Why Denial
Does Not Work

WHEN I DENY THE BODY, the world, or any aspect of my experience, I confiscate a portion of the identity I am here to transform. I cannot transform what I feel compelled to deny. As long as fear is present—and all denial is fear-based—transformation is impossible.

Denial is the quickest way toward dissociation between ego and spirit. While ego seems to intrude upon spirit, it is more appropriately seen as an overlay, or a mask. If I see only the mask, I will not see who my brother is; if he sees only the mask, he will not see me. This is not an identity problem, but a problem of perception.

My challenge is not to make the ego into an enemy, but to learn to look behind the mask of perception to see my innocence and yours. I am not here to change myself or you, or divide myself or you into good and bad pieces, but only to see the power of my beliefs at work.

This is an interesting purpose, is it not?

Unfortunately, my attempt to become responsible for my thoughts and actions disintegrates into endless episodes of guilt. Guilt is my defense against the truth.

Clearly, I do not come to innocence by beating myself up, nor will I come to it by denying my capacity for attack. I come to innocence by witnessing my attack and finding its source. I need to hear the call for love where it originates in myself. I need to look at the separation squarely.

It is absurd to see the separation cosmologically or developmentally. It is not something that happened in the past. It is something that happens right now. Right now I choose to see my innocence and yours or I choose to deny it in both of us. Denial never works. It simply recycles our experience so that we can be free to choose again.

Every time we deny something, we have to affirm something else. We have to take sides. We have to choose the positive over the negative or right over wrong. This is a moralistic game that goes on indefinitely. For, everything I deny comes back to me to look at.

The world of time that we know results directly from our need to choose between one thing and another or one person and another. When we become aware of our judgments, they cease to have power to create our reality. And then time as we know it becomes more permeable, more elastic. Its rigid laws begin to bend and shake.

Only our dualistic concepts and the judgments they provoke create the perception of time. Without concepts and judgments, time cannot exist, except as a series of present moments, each of which asks the same question: "would I separate or join?"

Recognizing this, I can have no other process

but witnessing or observing the choice I make moment to moment. That is the process of undoing what I have done. That is the destruction of the overlay, the dismantling of the world I have made out of my belief in separation and my fear of joining.

Erroneously, I think my problem lies in making the wrong choice. But that is absurd. There can be no wrong choices. Every choice is an opportunity to learn, so how could it be wrong? For instance, the choice to separate produces certain unsavory results, but let me not berate myself about this or I will just establish myself as a victim. Likewise, the choice to join produces certain ecstatic results, but let me not feel too much pride. In holding on to ecstasy, I will lose it.

I am neither the doer nor the one who is done to. I am only the witness, the one who sees good and evil, high and low, hot and cold. Except where I choose one over the other, I do not belong to the world of duality. I am the witness. I am the one who encompasses both. The opposites dwell within me and in me become whole.

Yet let me identify with one side and try to bring it to wholeness and I will not succeed. The very attempt to join one to the other by taking sides is preposterous.

As I deepen in my observation, I realize that there is no choice between good and evil, right and wrong, you and me, because these two are not real. These two are given their reality through my judgment and my choice. When I cease to judge, the need for choice dissolves. There are not two, but one.

One cannot reach the unity through denial unless one denies everything. So also, one cannot reach the unity through acceptance unless one accepts everything. Preference and partiality are innately dualistic and conflict-ridden. If I choose to accept here and deny there, I cannot experience the essential unity of all things.

Self with a small s cannot become Self with a capital S until there is no further need to choose between self and other. All lessons are therefore horizontal lessons, lessons of relationship. The vertical path, the ascent to God, cannot begin until I see God in myself and in my brother.

As long as there is one person I refuse to accept, how can I ascend? How can I enter the kingdom of Heaven? How can I who judge enter the place that is free of judgment?

I know only one answer. By taking responsibility for my judgments! By seeing them, accepting them, and asking for forgiveness. That is all I can do.

The Holy Spirit must do the rest. How he does it I don't know. He is the arbiter between the world of unity and the world of duality. When we give our judgments to Him, he returns them to us free of guilt. Then we can see them calmly, without fear of punishment. Then we can forgive ourselves. Then we can forgive each other. That is the blessing He holds for us. But we must have the courage to ask for it.

Christ
and Anti-Christ

THE WORLD WE LIVE IN seems to be a battle-ground between two great forces. In the past these forces have been labeled as the forces of good and the forces of evil, but those words no longer adequately characterize the nature of the conflict, nor the arena in which it occurs.

Both Christ and Anti-Christ live within the mind of every man and woman. Christ is the collective Spirit, the force for love and joining. Anti-Christ is the collective ego, the force of fear and separation. Christ liberates. Anti-Christ binds. Christ trusts his brother and sets him free to make mistakes and learn with perfect confidence in the outcome. Anti-Christ distrusts his brother's motives, seeks to influence his choice, and lives in constant fear of betrayal.

Anti-Christ preaches the end of the world through divine retribution. It says that those who believe will be saved, and that those who do not believe will perish. Its message is fear-based and its salvation is only for the chosen few. Christ offers salvation for all here and now. It places no price on the goal, and gives the gift freely to all who request it. It seeks no converts, respects free will, and lives with quiet conviction that the choice for God will be made by all sooner or later.

Anti-Christ sees ego, body and world as evil and preaches denial as a path to God. Christ sees ego, body and world as limited creations that open to love through acceptance and prayer. One would punish and blame. The other would forgive. Anti-Christ believes in Armageddon. Christ accepts the Atonement. One lives in a closed system, based on control and predictability. The other lives in an open system, where change is everpresent and respected as a force for good.

These two forces seem to be opposites, yet that is not so. The Anti-Christ cannot contain the Christ for it is exclusive by nature, cultivates enemies and does not know how to share. But the Christ invariably contains the Anti-Christ because it is inclusive by nature, practices forgiveness and reconciliation and has perfect faith in its own wholeness.

It seems that these forces move together in a vast collective drama, beyond the reach of our individual minds, but it can be rightfully said that the drama takes place only in our own minds. There we castigate some dark part of ourselves or we accept it as a necessary part of our wholeness. There we project our fear and exclude our brother, or we recognize it and reach for our brother's hand.

It seems to be a choice, yet it is only so for those who choose their own pain. Darkness chooses against light, but light cannot choose against darkness. It merely includes it, welcomes it, loves it. And so the darkness is shined away.

The light that opposes darkness is not light, but another form of darkness. Truth does not oppose falsehood. It waits patiently, quietly, yet with open arms.

The part of us that would attack evil binds us to the wheel of suffering. Yet that does not make that part of us evil. To reject any aspect of ourselves or others is a repudiation of our own wholeness. To the forces of apparent evil threateningly arraigned against us, love is the only answer. This is not such an easy lesson, but we will learn it yet.

Learning it means that we accept the Atonement for ourselves. It means that we embrace ourselves and release our brothers and sisters. It means that we let no obstacle stand between ourselves and God. That is the triumph of Christ. That is the teaching of our brother Jesus.

Remembering
to Laugh

A S LONG AS I FEEL that I have been injured, I can justify my dissatisfaction with you, with God, and with the world. I do not need elaborate defense systems to insure my unhappiness. A single grievance will do.

My friend Robert Ferre says that there is no path to happiness. Happiness itself is the path. As good spiritual students, we allow for happiness, but we look for it in the future. That way we can work hard on ourselves and really appreciate happiness when we get it. We try to seek happiness by holding onto our unhappiness. We seek to sacrifice our way into heaven. Of course, it doesn't work.

The only thing that stands between us and our happiness is our unhappiness. That is the wound we proudly show. It is our battle scar. It justifies our anger, our guilt, and our shame. It helps us hold onto our grievances.

The wound will not heal until we give it permission to. And that permission can only be given now. You see, it doesn't matter if we've been terribly unhappy all our lives. We decide to be happy now, not yesterday or tomorrow. Look at Scrooge. He did it and we can too.

Making a simple decision like that isn't very spiritually provocative. I mean, if it came after meditating alone in a cave for ten years, then maybe it would have some punch behind it. But just deciding right now to be happy? You must be kidding right? Well, as funny as Robert is — and I assure you he is very funny— I don't think he is kidding. Also, if you try it, you might find it is a little harder than you think. In fact, if you try it long enough, you might realize that it isn't that much easier than meditating in a cave!

The difference is that happiness pays immediate dividends. When you succeed, you get instant feedback. Of course, you get instant feedback when you don't succeed too!

I like Robert's method, because the goal and the process are exactly the same. So if I am unhappy trying to be happy than I'm obviously not giving myself permission to be happy. You see, there's no out!

Sooner or later, I begin to realize that my real challenge is to learn to be happy being unhappy. Have you ever tried that? I mean here I am being miserable, I might as well enjoy it right? I'll just give myself permission to get into this. Let's see, now what can I do to make myself more miserable?

Ram Dass used to talk about the importance of having a cosmic sense of humor. When life deals you nothing but lemons, you open a lemonade stand. What else can you do with a bunch of lemons?

When the goal and the process become one and the same, every mistake becomes an experience not only of correction, but also of At-one-ment. In the past, we used to beat ourselves for making mistakes. Now we celebrate the mistakes by learning to laugh at ourselves.

I've had a lot of lessons in my life, but lately I've begun to realize that the only real lesson I need to learn is how not to take myself so seriously. Last night, my friend Kevin reminded me that *A Course in Miracles* does not need me to protect it. Now how many times have I said that to others? Well, I guess we only teach what we need to learn. Anyway, thank you, Kevin.

Thanks for reminding me that every response I want to make to perceived injustice really is a Quixotic campaign against the shadows in my own mind. Those who anger me are ghosts passing in the night. The only reality they have is to show me my own fears.

The truth is that it's really funny to see myself getting all dressed up in my designer armor, mounting my faithful steed "Justification" and riding out in the night. I've never seen anything more hysterical than a half-bald, overweight, middle-aged man attacking a bunch of windmills. I mean, thank God there wasn't much wind that night!

My friend Fran knows that she's finally connected with me when she gets me to laugh. Thanks Fran. Thanks Robert. Thanks Kevin. Thanks for reminding me to laugh.

The Eternal Flame

WE ARE ALL KEEPERS of the flame. We all want to be special, but our strength does not lie in our specialness; it lies in our equality.

Those we accept as our teachers just reinforce our specialness. But our real teachers challenge our specialness. When we recognize their gift to us, we cannot help but be deeply grateful.

We are all keepers of the flame. Each one of us sees a portion of truth not seen by others. When we really understand this and surrender to it, our lives change.

At first, we are invested in our specialness. We think it is the only way that we will get the support and appreciation we want. But the more we seek specialness, the unhappier we get. Specialness is an attack, and so it invariably meets with opposition. Then, we feel that we must defend ourselves against others who resent or otherwise feel invalidated by our specialness.

When we lay down this false burden, we feel incredible relief. So much of the energy we invested in defensive, self-protective rituals is freed to serve our happiness and the greater good. Doors we could not find before now open to us. Opportunities that went by quietly unperceived now walk up to us and shake our hands.

When I stop attacking, love finds me. I don't have to seek for it any more. When I accept my equality with you, a joining occurs that was not possible as long as we each claimed our specialness. Now the At-one-ment ceases to be an abstract concept. Now we see the Christ in one another. Now the body of Christ is born.

I have spent the last several years focused on the issue of bringing Miracles students together into conscious community and communion. Over and over, whenever we join, our egos pop up with a vengeance. Each one of us looks for special attention, for a special role, for special recognition. Then our judgments of one another plug up the holy space between us. Then we feel wounded by one another and cut off again.

At every Miracles gathering, the Separation is re-enacted. And we throw up our hands and cry out for help. And before we know it, the Holy Spirit's answer comes through one of our brothers or sisters, often from the one we think least likely to offer us insight. The answer comes and we feel a warm wave of peace move through our hearts as we remember to laugh and to love.

Every time we rise in specialness, we feel the weight of its pull, as it drags us to earth. It offers to lift us above our brothers, but it does not tell us about "the fall." We always find out the hard way.

We do not ascend in truth save with our sister's hand. What lifts us up must uplift her too or the force of gravity will humble us yet again.

Each moment offers us a choice of whether to

separate or join. That is the only choice we have faced before and the only choice we will ever face. Unfortunately, we keep forgetting the outcome. We do not remember the pain of separation or the bliss of joining. That is why we have come to this place together, to help each other remember, to learn to take each other's hand, to join the body of truth we never left except in the loneliness of our own dream.

PART TEN

The Teaching Poems

*"The choice you
must make is not
whether or not
to give up the world,
but whether or not
to give up
your unhappiness."*

————•————

The Teaching Poems

The Way Out of Conflict:
A Message from Jesus

I

The ideas of others do not apply to you.
The experience of others belongs
only to them. Be with your own ideas.
Rest in your own experience.

But understand that what troubles you
shows you what you need to learn.
Every person who opposes you
is your teacher.

Remember, truth cannot be threatened.
If you feel threatened,
look at your fear. Don't try
to make the apparition real.

II

Those who say they know more than you
proclaim their own ignorance.
Those who seek to convert you
betray their own doubts.

That is the nature of the world.
It is not necessary to oppose it.
Simply understand it
and go about your business.

A loving person does not perpetuate
attack in any guise,
nor does he close his eyes
to people's motives.

His unconditional acceptance
of each person
enables him to discriminate clearly
without taking sides.

III

If understanding is your goal
set your judgments aside
and look at them
one by one, as you make them.

Then you will understand
that what prevents you from
entering love's presence
blocks others too.

Seeing the obstacle in others,
you learn to gently
step around it
and offer love instead.

IV

People look for specialness
because they do not trust themselves.
If they do not trust themselves,
how can they trust each other?

This is not a time for special teachers,
teachings, or techniques.
It is a time for opening the heart.
It is a time for listening within.

Peace is the only barometer of truth.
And not a single one of you
can read the barometer
in another's heart.

Your ego will always be in conflict
with other egos. Your job
is to observe this, not to try
to make the ego go away.

Love that depends on agreement
is not love, but attack.
Love welcomes the dissenter
into its limitless embrace.

Don't let words divide you
into two separate camps.
There is only one camp.
There is only one plan for the Atonement.

V

I assure you there is justice for everyone.
Every mistake is brought to truth.
There is nothing here
you need to protect or defend.

Listen to each other deeply
without needing to agree or disagree
and you will know where
the voice of truth originates.

I do not ask you to become wiser
than your brother or sister,
but merely to discover
your absolute equality.

Every perception of inequality
requires forgiveness.
It is that simple.
Further discussion is unnecessary.

VI

You think that you are separate
from one another,
but you are all
in the same boat.

Some people complain about the vessel.
Others try to escape it.
Both are clever ways of getting
more deeply enmeshed in conflict.

Until you accept the boat
for what it is,
it cannot take you
to the other side.

I have said many times:
leave the means to the Holy Spirit.
The process of enlightenment belongs to Him,
not to you.

VII

All you can do is understand the goal
and commit to it, moment to moment.
Every time you commit to the goal,
the means to reach it will be found.

The choice you must make
is not whether or not to give up the world,
but whether or not
to give up your unhappiness.

When you give up your grievances,
you stop projecting your anger and guilt
    on the world.
And then the world is not
the same place it once seemed to be.

VIII

If separation is an illusion,
then everything is perfect
the way it is.
This is love's vision.

I have told you that if you open your heart
to your brother, you will receive
everything you ever sought from him
through less congenial means.

IX

Everyone and everything
that comes to you in your life
is part of the teaching
if you are willing to accept it.

This is not a path of denial.
When I ask you to deny the illusion,
I am simply asking you to change your mind
about what you find painful.

Once you change your mind,
the pain goes away.
This demonstrates to you
that it was never real to begin with.

X

My words are a call to awaken,
but do not think you will awaken
without your brother, nor underestimate
your power to set him free.

In the end, he will decide for himself,
but you can make that decision
easier for him, and he
can do the same for you.

Without your brother,
you are like a man walking on one leg.
It's not impossible,
but it's not very efficient.

To be alone is essential,
but never sufficient.
No matter how solitary you become,
you can't escape your brother's call for help.

To try to do so is foolish.
Indeed, it is his call for help
which forces you to look
at your own anger and guilt.

XI

Many false prophets promise
easier and faster ways to truth,
but the steps they would skip
lengthen the journey.

Watch out for short cuts.
There's plenty of time.
All projections must be seen and acknowledged
before they can be withdrawn.

XII

There is no path to truth
that does not move through the mind's shadows,
or sink down into the heart
to teach the doubter how to bless.

You cannot be a channel for the Body of Christ
so long as you see any member of that Body
as an enemy
or an interference in your work.

But take heart. The way
has been laid out before you,
using the props you have chosen
for the journey.

Your path is as certain
as its destination,
and your salvation as sure
as your ability to love.

The Infinite Embrace

There is nothing other than
your own experience,

no matter what anyone else says about it,
no matter what you think or feel about it,

nothing outside it,
nothing inside it,
nothing before it,
and nothing after it.

Your experience is the universe you live in:
your heaven, your hell,
and all the borderlands that mediate between.

Your experience cannot be tampered with,
discounted, or justified.
It is merely what it is.

When seeking God with words and concepts
comes to an end,
when there is nothing to give
and nothing to receive
other than what spontaneously gives
and receives itself,

when there is no enlightenment
or unenlightenment,
we rest in the Holy Place.

We do not know how we got here,
because every journey we made
took us away from this Place,
yet we are here together, heart to heart,
face to face.

We are here always,
as long as we have nothing
to prove or dis-prove,
as long as we have no need to evaluate others
or ourselves.

Truth needs no support.
Falsehood needs no opposition.
Now, in this moment,
is the love in which we rest
simply, unconditionally,
without definition, without measure:

this I which is you also,
this you which is also I,
this place where we meet
and recognize each other
as brother, as sister,
the infinite embrace.

Fire of the Heart

I

The shaman's dance is done
Morning has broken
with passion, far beyond
these white hills
where dawn is muted
by clouds.

Here, fatherless,
in a sun-forsaken land
we settle in
like wind-blown snow
brought to the brow
of a mountain,

or like a stray hawk
that commands
the summit,
only to fall back down
the wind, as winter
lands at the nadir

and the dance of light begins.

II

Before men had fire, days were arduous
and nights empty and dark.

The stench of flesh mingled with the breath
and might made the marriage bed.

Fire gave men a warm place to rest
and a hearth to tell stories.

It built a bridge between men.
It was an instrument of reverie.

III

When I was little
my mother was angry.
I went to my father
for protection,
but he was as afraid
as I was.

I withdrew deep in the cave,
far away from
where the fire burned.
Boys tried to provoke me,
throwing stones, calling me names,
but I remained hidden.

I dreamed of fire. I played
with the hidden fire.
I cried hidden tears.

Women sought me out
near the cave's entrance,
but I moved awkwardly
between the safety of the dark
and the warm winged imagery
of the flames.

Only recently, have I taken
my place by the fire,
telling stories
long into the night.

Only now has the wild one,
the creature of shadows
come home.

IV

It is,
as has been said.

Ego cannot vanquish ego.
Something else is needed.

Without fire,
mind cannot be purified.

Without pain, the wound
cannot be named.

My doubts now belong to the flames.
Also my desires and fears.

I stand watch long into the night.

Everything that is not of the fire
must be given over to the fire.

That is the purification ritual.
That is the end of guilt.

V

Without the fire, there are gods,
but they remain aloof.
Without the fire, there is truth
but no one who can understand it.

It was different at Gethsemane.
Women were weeping,
and light rose in the dark sky
so pale and unsymmetrical
you could barely see
the soul leave the body.

A stillness settled in upon the land,
a stillness so deep that even now
men are crucified by
the sound of their own voices
shifting in the wind.

VI

Darkness always comes first
to the hearts of women and men.
The temptation to possess

darkens the mind with shadows.
As desire grows,
so does fear.

This morning, light is stretched
in the beauty of snow
like an innocent dancer.

Shapes curl within shapes,
lights within lights,
dreams within dreams.

A snowman stands the lookout
unaware of the pool of blood
that gathers at his feet.

Then he shifts into motion,
whirling on one leg,
like a dervish.

The likelihood of a breakthrough
is slim, but the dance
intensifies.

In the Middle-East,
we mosey up to war: the cold feel of steel
against blood-stained hands.

Beauty's legacy dies first in the mind.
At night children and adults sleep with TV
and wake to news

of bodies stretched out in the sand.

VII

You cannot rescue anyone
from the flames
before he is ready to come out.

Those imprisoned in the ice
of separation
need the heat to melt it.

Those who have attacked others
need to learn
to ask for love.

Those who have been neglected or abused
need to learn
to give it.

VIII

Try to decide for others
and the flame scalds.
Let them decide for you
and you shiver.

A timid fire cannot
keep itself going.
A fire that rages
burns itself out.

Sooner or later,
every role must be disclaimed,
every thought that runs shy of love
must be surrendered.

XI

Caught in a cross-fire,
each tries to extinguish
the other's flame.

Women and children are maimed.
Soldiers shoot their own men.

Crossfires are perverse.
It is the nature of fire
to rise upward, not to move
from side to side.

Take the flame back inside
and you threaten no one.

Neither give offense nor take it.
Burn steady. See steady.
Love steady.

Others will come and stand in your light.
Let them come and go.

They will light their torches
at your doorstep. Let them.
It will not help them.
It will not hurt you.

Each must find his light
and nurture it. If he doesn't,
he will die in the darkness.

There is no escape from the ring of fire.
In it dance devils and angels.

In it the bird of love
is burned to death
and rises from its ashes.

This happens many times. There is
no end to it. There is no end
to the fire of the heart.

XII

Hell is not a place
but a state of mind
made by self-pity and regret.

The fire of hell is poorly tended.
Its light is eerie, inconstant,
filtered by judgment.

In it, phantoms arise
and brothers are slain,
taken for ghosts with malicious intent.

The guilty cannot make the journey
through the flames
till they relinquish their pain.

When they do, their time in hell
is just a memory of self-abuse
which they must learn to forgive.

XIII

Men think that it is God who punishes them,
but, in truth, God cares not
for their plots and counterplots.

God cares only for the still mind
and the heart that sings
simple songs of welcome.

God has been used by men,
but men have rarely allowed themselves
to be used by God.

To be used by God
does not mean to be used by men,
but it does mean giving up personal agendas.

It means giving up control.
Those who care only for their own results
carry the ego's mission of guilt.

They hold the rock that holds the world
in chains. They carelessly set fire
to the tree of life.

XIV

The fire of the heart
rages and sputters
when I try to manipulate you
or allow you to pressure me.

Holding the heart aloof
just dulls the pain.

The fire in each being
must be brought under control
before its light can shine through.

No one becomes a light-bearer
until the ego-fabricated assumptions
fall away.

As the emotions are refined,
the defenses built against love
come tumbling down.

When the teaching of darkness
is complete, light dawns.

XV

I am sick of the idea of owning anything.

When resources are contested,
violation has already occurred
and must be mended.

You do not set sail into a stiff wind
with a torn sail.

We are not here to appropriate others
or be taken as slaves.

The power to wound cannot be contained.
It eventually returns home
to the mind that wills it.

XVI

The action of light
in the mind's darkness
is dreamlike.

But once you lose the thread
of light, everything
happens by tunnel vision.

The power of thoughts to oppress
is equalled only by their power
to put the dreamer to sleep.

At the witching hour, I see
the proud and the greedy
slipping to their knees.

Now they know for sure
that all injury
is self injury.

Where thought begins, beauty falters.
Strange flowers grow
along the footpaths

leading down to the old tombs
where the animals winter
away from the cold.

When the ground warms up,
the dirt will fall from our eyes,
and the water of guilt

will spill from our lips.
It will be a virgin birth:
the kiss of fire and ice

in the spring thaw.

XVII

It is all a play of mind
what happens from here out:
the long green thumb of hope
jammed in the dikes of some
nuclear winter.

Lies like flies
fester around a pile of dung
as Wall Street winks
and taxpayers ante up.

Soon the kids will be drafted
and every accident
assigned some intention
it does not have.

Weapons that boggle the mind
will explode as infants sleep,
while men in grey suits
read well practiced lines
in front of microphones.

This war is no different than any other.
Conflict is held together
by the thoughts and actions
of each side, an argument
fought with live amunition.

XVIII

No one can teach your grief
to play,
yet it must learn how.

A wounded man
cannot be taught how to sing,
yet sing he must.

A man who refuses to sing
will not find his brother.
His wife and children

will be an affliction.
He will feel imprisoned
like a caged bird.

A man in prison rarely sings,
but sing he must
or he will forget his wings.

XIX

Eyes peer through the flames,
eyes no one has seen,
heart-red eyes
drinking the moment in.

It is a long way from this place
to the cave.

On Tarot card number eighteen
the dogs of worry
guard the inner sanctum
where the dead sleep.

Growling and nipping at my heels,
they tried to intimidate me,
but it is over now.

I have walked through that tunnel
of shame and blame.
I have watched the hidden hands
red and forgiving,
lift the long night.

Now stronger tissue seals the wound,
and I am wound-bred, a shaman
dancing with fiery wings
around the funeral pyre.

The Door
to the
House of Love

There is a door in the mind
that opens
with acceptance
and closes
with judgment of any kind.

There is a door in the heart
that opens with trust
and closes
when fear of any kind
is felt.

There is a door in the body
which opens as we relax
and closes
when we tense up
in self defense.

There is a door
that opens to grace
and closes in disgrace,
a door that bids you come in
and a door
that shuts you out.

In this house
there are many doors.
Some are open.
Some are closed.
Some are just beginning to open.
Some are just beginning to close.

Some doors close behind us
when we step through them;
others open before us
as we cross the threshold.

Nobody knows what the door is,
or when it will appear.

Sometimes it seems not to be a door,
yet it opens.
Sometimes it seems to be a door,
yet no one can enter through it.

When the door is open,
the fact that it is a door
is of no significance.

It could be a window, a room, or sun
pouring through a window
in a room.

Sometimes I look for God
and cannot find Him.
I stand unsteady
in the darkness.

I know there is a door,
but I cannot see it.
I grapple for it,
but my hands move in vain
along the wall.

I know there is a door
but I cannot find it.
In the pitch black,
there is the smallest of lights.

I move toward it;
it forgives me.

I reach for it;
it forgives you.

I hold it in my hands;
it blesses the world
I have judged.

There is a door in my heart
containing an ocean
of silence,
a sky full of flying birds.

I move upward with them
and downward to the place
of shadows.

I hear the song of sorrow
and the joy that comes
after tears.

Until the door closes
the boundaries
of the body and mind
are undefined.

Birds fly out from the heart
and dance in the sky.
Light dances in the eyes
and falls where the feet fall.

Until the door closes,
all needs are met,
all dances danced,
all poems written
all prayers prayed.

Until the door closes
everyone lives with me;
when it closes I am alone.

And I know
that all of this is okay:
high and low,
pain and joy,
light and darkness.

And I know that I
am not who I think I am
and you are not
who I think you are.

And I know that the door will open
as I begin to trust,
and that it will close
when I am afraid.

And I know it is okay to be afraid.
And I know it is okay to feel
whatever I feel.

And I know that it is okay
for the door to open and close,
open and close,
open and close,
until it no longer matters
whether it is open or closed
because the place it opens to
is the same place
it closes in.

And then I will relax deeply
in my body
and in my feelings
and in my thoughts,

and my spirit
will remain in its resting place.

*P*aul Ferrini is the author of a number of books and tapes which help us integrate spirituality into our daily lives. Paul's work is heart-centered and experiential. It empowers us to create a life of dignity that honors our inmost talents and abilities. It encourages us to open our hearts to one another and share who we are. A student and teacher of *A Course in Miracles*, Paul Ferrini is the editor and publisher of *Miracles Magazine*, an international magazine linking together Course students worldwide. Paul's "Joining Together" conferences, retreats and workshops have helped thousands of students deepen their practice of forgiveness and open their hearts to the Christ presence in themselves and others.

The Miracles Community Network

The Miracles Community Network (MCN) is a non-profit organization dedicated to bringing together students of *A Course in Miracles* in communion, community and meaningful dialogue. Toward that end, MCN sponsors conferences, workshops and retreats that bring together Miracles students and teachers from all over the world to share ideas, Miracles stories, and to deepen our understanding and practice of the forgiveness process.

The Miracles Community Network (MCN) welcomes as members Course students and organizations committed to an open and loving discussion of the issues facing our worldwide community. MCN appreciates the diversity within our community and welcomes it. It repudiates the concept that there is only one "right" way to study or practice the Course. Indeed, by encouraging a variety of perspectives through its publications and community events, MCN offers students the information they need to make choices about their own study and practice of the Course.

The Miracles Community Network encourages members to collaborate on a wide range of projects that utilize their skills and creative talents. Writers, musicians, photographers, computer programmers, body work practitioners, designers, dancers, etc. have participated in MCN events and projects. Many members have gone on to collaborate on songs, articles, books and tapes. There has been a great creative outpouring and a wonderful process of joining.

We invite your participation on our collaborative projects and community-building activities. For more information please write:

The Miracles Community Network
P.O. Box 418
Santa Fe, NM 87504-0418

Heartways Press

"Integrating Spirituality into Daily Life"
Books by Paul Ferrini

- **The Twelve Steps of Forgiveness**

    This book is a practical manual for healing ourselves and our relationships. It gives us a step by step process for moving through our fears, projections, judgments, and guilt so that we can take responsibility for creating the life we want. With great gentleness, we learn to embrace our lessons and to find equality with others. A must read for all in recovery and others seeking spiritual wholeness.

    128 pp. paper 5½ x 8½ ISBN 1-879159-10-4 $10.00

- **The Circle of Atonement**

  This book explores a healing process in which we confront our deep-seated guilt and fear, bringing love and forgiveness to the wounded child within. By surrendering our judgments of self and others, we overcome feelings of separation and dismantle co-dependent patterns that restrict our self-expression and ability to give and receive love. A must-read for all students of *A Course in Miracles* and others looking for spiritual direction beyond recovery.

  224 pp. paper 5½ x 8½ ISBN 1-879159-06-6 $12.00

- **The Bridge To Reality**

  A Heart-centered Approach to *A Course in Miracles* and the Process of Inner Healing. Sharing from his experiences as a teacher and student of The Course, the author emphasizes self-acceptance and forgiveness as cornerstones of spiritual practice. Beautifully presented with outquotes and photos, this book conveys the essence of The Course as it is lived in daily life.

  160 pp. paper 6 x 9 ISBN 1-879159-03-1 $12.00

- **From Ego To Self**

  108 illustrated affirmations designed to offer you a new way of viewing conflict situations so that you can overcome negative thinking and bring more energy, faith and optimism into your life.

  128 pp. paper 6x5 ISBN 1-879159-01-5 $10.00

- **Virtues Of The Way**

  A lyrical work of contemporary scripture reminiscent of the Tao Te Ching. Beautifully illustrated, this inspirational book helps you cultivate the spiritual values required to fulfill your creative purpose and live in harmony with others.

  64 pp. paper 5½ x 8½ ISBN 1-879159-02-3 $7.50

- **The Body Of Truth**

  A crystal clear introduction to many of the key concepts discussed in A Course in Miracles and other universal teachings. This book traces all forms of suffering to negative attitudes and false beliefs, which we have the ability to transform.

  64 pp. paper 5½ x 8½ ISBN 1-879159-02-3 $7.50

- **Available Light**

  Inspirational, passionate poems dealing with the work of inner integration, love and relationships, death and re-birth, loss and abundance, life purpose and the reality of spiritual vision. A must read for all seeking self-actualization.

  128 pp. paper 5½ x 8½ ISBN 1-879159-05-8 $10.00

Miracles Magazine

An international quarterly magazine for teachers and students of *A Course in Miracles*. Each issue includes inspirational miracles stories, in-depth articles and interviews with Course spokespeople around the world, beautiful artwork and photography, poetry, events calendar and much more. Single issue: $9.00. One-year subscription: $25.00.

Heartways Music

"Music that stirs the heart and uplifts the soul!"
Cassettes by Paul Ferrini & Michael Gray

• The Circle of Healing

by Paul Ferrini & Michael Gray

It's finally available. The meditation and healing tape
that many of you have been requesting for months is
now here. This gentle mediation opens the heart to
love's presence and extends that love to all the beings
in your experience. A powerful tape with inspirational piano accompaniment by Michael Gray.
ISBN # 1-879159-08-2 $10.00

• Healing the Wounded Child

A potent healing tape that accesses old feelings of
pain, fragmentation, self-judgment and separation
and brings them into the light of conscious awareness
and acceptance. Side two includes hauntingly beautiful "inner child" reading from The Bridge to Reality
with piano accompaniment by Michael Gray.
ISBN # 1-879159-11-2 $10.00

- **Forgiveness: Returning to the Original Blessing**
  A Self Healing tape that helps us accept and learn from the mistakes we have made in the past. By letting go of our judgments and ending our ego-based search for perfection, we can bring our darkness to the light, dissolving anger, guilt, and shame. Piano accompaniment by Michael Gray.
  ISBN # 1-879159-12-0 $10.00

Heartways Press
ORDER FORM

NAME_____

ADDRESS_____

CITY_____STATE_____ZIP_____

PHONE_____

Books

The Wisdom of the Self ($12.00)   _____

The Twelve Steps of Forgiveness ($10.00) _____

The Circle of Atonement ($12.00)   _____

The Bridge to Reality ($12.00)   _____

From Ego to Self ($10.00)   _____

Virtues of the Way ($7.50)   _____

The Body of Truth ($7.50)   _____

Available Light ($10.00)   _____

Tapes

The Circle of Healing ($10.00)   _____

Healing the Wounded Child ($10.00)   _____

Forgiveness: Returning to the Original Blessing

       ($10.00)   _____

Miracles Magazine

Single Issue ($9.00)   _____

1 year subscription ($25.00)   _____

2 year subscription ($45.00)   _____

Shipping

($2.00 for first item, $.50 each additional item.

Add additional $1.00 for first class postage.)   _____

New Mexico residents please add 6.125% sales tax. _____

TOTAL $ _____

Send Order To: Heartways Press
                   P.O. Box 418
                   Santa Fe, NM 87504-0418
                   Tel: 505/989-3656

Please allow 1-2 weeks for delivery